T0006753

# YEAR-ROUND EDIBLE GARDENING

# YEAR-ROUND EDIBLE GARDENING

## GROWING VEGETABLES AND HERBS, INSIDE OR OUTSIDE, IN EVERY SEASON

*Lena Israelsson*

Skyhorse Publishing

# CONTENTS

*A motley August harvest: tomatoes,
Borlotti beans, and chili peppers.*

# THESE DAYS, I GARDEN ALL YEAR

IN THE PAST, my gardening season used to last five months. Now it spans twelve months, and I've tripled my yield. I harvest tender leaves under the spring sun, and move on to sweet tomatoes and chubby cucumbers in the summer. I feast on Japanese mizuna cabbage and root vegetables well into late fall.

Finally, winter is when kale is at its peak, and mâche—also called lamb's lettuce or corn lettuce—and winter purslane (known too as miner's lettuce), are doing great. But for other plants, their best days are behind them, whether they're buried in snow or not. So, this is the time when I head indoors. Here, new adventures await in the form of microgreens, herbs, and hydroculture. When all is said and done, every season gives rise to its own kind of joy. And that is why I'm a year-round gardener.

## IT ALL STARTED IN CHINA

Eighteen years ago, I was in northern China studying their method of intensive cultivation, which encompasses year-round gardening. I not only learned how to maximize yields without depleting the soil, but also how to prolong the growing season by, among other things, choosing the right types of plants.

Since then, I've supplemented my "toolbox" with heated frames, tunnel greenhouses, mobile tunnels and, last but not least, indoor gardening. Most important, I've test-grown huge amounts of plants to find out which are the toughest. *Year-Round Edible Gardening* is the result of these experiences.

## GROUNDLESS FEAR

You'll find a comprehensive "cheat sheet" (on p. 14) of annual plantings for the kitchen garden, with information about everything from planting to cold hardiness. Among the 66 plants listed in this sheet, 56 of them will tolerate light frost or a few degrees below freezing. Some plants' flavors are even improved by a touch of frost. In other words, our phobic fear of frost is groundless.

The idea behind the cheat sheet is that with it, you should be able to plan your garden and combine plants in order to prolong the growing season. It'll work just as well with a pallet rim* and vegetable patch as with pots on the balcony.

I won't claim that everyone who reads this book will turn into a constant gardener. However, I'll be happy if some of you are able to lengthen the growing season by a few months. Why not set aside

---

* Pallet rims are common add-ons for pallets in the European Market: http://www.gkprodukter.se/pallkrage.html

*Organic matter—this is what the ground needs to provide me with more than a single harvest.*

a garden bed for the cold-hardiest plants, such as kale, mâche, and winter purslane, and grow them in a plastic "caterpillar" tunnel? That way you could get to harvest vegetables at Christmastime.

## FOR GARDENERS ALL OVER THE COUNTRY

I'd like all gardeners in Sweden to be able to use this book. That's why each season's section begins with weather facts pertaining to every area of the country. My statistics come from the government agency SMHI (Swedish Meteorological and Hydrological Institute), and they show the normal range from 1961 to 1990 (the only years for which data is available).

However, we're also aware that global warming has brought about higher temperatures since then; SMHI states that they have risen by about 34°F (1°C). Keep this in mind when you check the figures!

If we fail to stop emitting greenhouse gases, temperatures will rise by about 40°F to 43°F (4°C to 6°C) by the year 2100, according to SMHI, and the area most affected will be the north of Sweden. At the same time, levels of precipitation are increasing by 30 to 50 percent, so we will have to contend with more plant diseases and destructive pests.

Naturally, it's impossible to feel happy about these statistics, even if they do mean that our growing season is longer. We're headed straight toward a global catastrophe, which is going to make parts of the globe uninhabitable.

But we know one thing for sure: It's always good for the environment to grow your own food, and over twelve months rather than five.

*Lena Israelsson*

9

*The key to success is staggered sowing, and to always have new plants on hand.*

# PLANNING THE HARVEST

## NOW IS THE TIME TO LAY THE GROUNDWORK FOR YEAR-ROUND GARDENING, AND WE AIM TO DOUBLE OR TRIPLE THE HARVEST.

FERTILE SOIL IS A PREREQUISITE FOR ALL CULTIVATION; it's possibly even vital if you garden throughout most of the year, since the soil is going to be more productive per square foot. Year-round gardening distinguishes itself from traditional gardening with four principles, the first and most important being *forward planning*. Without this step, you will have neither a fall nor a winter harvest. Forward planning is all about preparing for tomorrow. If you wish to harvest produce in late fall, planting for it in September will not work—it must to be done as early as in July or August. By the way, sowing just once per year is so typically Swedish. Make a habit of putting in several staggered plantings instead.

Forward planning also means having small starter plants at the ready. I force new plants as soon as I feel like it and have the time to do it, so they're available for planting when a spot opens up. The method of having young plants at one's disposal is unbeatable. My advice to anyone who wishes to prolong their growing season is to have forced plants on hand to fill in the gaps, which will stretch their harvest. Yes, I know, there will always be a few leftover plants. Go ahead and share them with other gardeners.

The second principle is to practice *intensive gardening;* i.e., to use all the different methods of intensive cultivation. This will maximize the harvest without depleting the soil, and without contributing to the emission of greenhouse gases.

Here are a few examples of intensive gardening: growing in raised beds, mulching with garden waste and/or garden fabric, interplanting, staggered sowing and fertilizing, and growing in tunnel greenhouses (poly-tunnels), cold frames, and low greenhouse tunnels (quick hoops). I'll go over all of these in more detail later on.

### WEATHER DETECTION

The third principle is *weather detection*—keeping an eye on the weather and following the forecast. Meteorological conditions are the only thing we year-round gardeners cannot control. But we are gamblers, and so we assume that our tomatoes will ripen and the cucumbers won't be washed away by the rain. And, fortunately, we're not without tools. Here are some of the most important implements at our disposal:

**A digital thermometer** is critical. You'll need one that displays information about minimum and maximum temperatures for both day and night times. Since the kitchen is the first and last room I'm in during the day, I have a thermometer at the kitchen window. A thermometer in the garden is just as important.

**Weather forecasts** are invaluable. Weather sites provide extended as well as hour-by-hour weather forecasts. Changes seldom happen

*There is no reason to waste space in pallet rims. Here, they're tightly packed.*

quickly, which is to our benefit. I'm not worried if it's 44.6°F (7°C) when I go to bed, since the likelihood of a 6 a.m. frost is just about zero.

**Garden records.** Well-organized individuals keep track of their plantings, sowings, harvests, the weather, etc. This is a good way to learn how plants respond to different weath-

er conditions. I find that photographic documentation is enough—that way I automatically get a date-stamp, too.

## SMART PLANT CHOICES

I have now reached the fourth principle, which is about making *smart plant choices*. Only grow produce that makes your mouth water when think-

**12**

*The first radishes … followed by Kalibos, a pointy—sometimes called "sweetheart"—cabbage.*

ing of it; that way you can be sure it will be used up. That's the most significant piece of advice I can give you. The second is to check the plants' rate of growth when you plan your yearly sowing. For example, planting parsnips before cabbage doesn't make sense, since both plants take a long time to grow. Instead, if you want two harvests, you'll have to combine a fast-growing plant with a slower developing one, like, say, arugula and kale. If your goal is three harvests, two plants need to be fast growers and one a slow developer.

Think in terms of hors d'oeuvre, entrée, and dessert. Begin with a fast-growing crop for starters, followed by a slower growing entrée. If you're lucky—and only if you live in the south of Sweden—you might be able to harvest a fast-grower for dessert.

It's also a good idea to go with early varieties, such as Nantes carrots. Only choose what we refer to as "storage" varieties if the carrots are meant for use at a later date. May I also suggest Little Gem, a miniature romaine lettuce that grows in record time and tastes amazing. This is my best hors d'oeuvre, next to sweetheart cabbage.

Another smart option is to grow "cut-and-come-again" varieties; those types are harvested

over and over during the better part of summer. Chard and parsley are the best examples. New growth will appear if you simply fertilize and harvest the plants regularly. You'll find more cut-and-come-again plants on the cheat sheet on p. 14.

Below, I provide examples on how to combine a quick-growing spring crop with a slower growing summer crop. I combine plants from the same botanical family as often as possible for the sake of proper crop rotation (p. 52).

You can check both a plant's growth rate and its cold-hardiness on the cheat sheet. With it, you can plan your garden so you'll have two, maybe even three harvests.

| QUICK SPRING CROP | SLOW SUMMER CROP |
| --- | --- |
| Cilantro | Endive |
| Arugula | Kale |
| Radish | White, red or pointy cabbage |
| Romaine lettuce | Corn |
| Watercress | Broccoli |
| Spinach | Leeks |

# YOUR COMPLETE CHEAT SHEET

**THE CHEAT SHEET THAT FOLLOWS IS THE CORE OF THIS BOOK. YOU CAN USE IT TO SELECT AND COMBINE PLANTS TO GROW BIGGER HARVESTS THAN YOU'VE EVER DREAMED OF. IN THE SPRING CHAPTER, YOU CAN READ ABOUT THE GENERAL RULES OF PLANTING. AFTER ALL, IT'S IN SPRING THAT WE'LL GET STARTED ON THE BIG SOWING.**

**THE CHEAT SHEET CONTAINS** all the information you'll need to maximize the harvest and/or pick more than one harvest. It will also come in handy when you organize your crop rotation (p. 52). I've included a few unusual plants—specimens that work exceptionally well in early spring and late fall.

However, before you dive head first into the cheat sheet, take a look at the chart opposite. There you'll find an explanation for the different column headings.

*The cheat sheet contains information about planting, fertilizing, and harvesting celery root and other plants....*

**Explanation of cheat sheet headings (p. 16–25).**

| COLUMN HEADING | EXPLANATION |
|---|---|
| Cold or Warm Weather Plant (C or W) | *Cold weather plants* are planted directly in the ground. Most will germinate at 41°F (5°C); they thrive in the Swedish summer and are cold-hardy down to a few degrees below freezing. *Warm weather plants* are started earlier, usually indoors, and are set out when nighttime temperatures are around 50°F (10°C)–53.6°F (12°C). They require a long, sunny summer; alternatively, they can be grown in a poly-tunnel or greenhouse. These plants are not cold-hardy. |
| Plant Spacing | These are approximate distances. The distance doesn't just depend on the plant, but also on plant type. Some lettuces span about 8" (20 cm) across in diameter, while others measure almost 12" (30 cm) in diameter. Check the seed packet for information, and don't skimp on the distance between the plants. |
| Row Spacing | You can narrow the row distance noted on the seed packet or in the book by about 20 percent if you're growing your plants in a pallet rim or other type of raised bed. The plant spacing width is all you need, since you won't be walking between the plants. |
| Planting Depth | General rule: A seed should be planted 4 to 5 times as deep as its seed's diameter. Seeds planted 0 to 0.08" deep need light to germinate. |
| Lowest Germination Temperature | This is the temperature required for the seed to germinate. You can check the soil's temperature with a regular thermometer; simply stick it in the ground. Seeds often grow even better if the soil's temperature is slightly higher. |
| Days to Maturity | Days from planting to harvest. |
| Start Indoors (SI) or Direct Sow (DS) | Some plants must be started indoors because they take a long time to mature. This means that they're planted in pots or pallets, either indoors or in a greenhouse/cold frame. Other seeds are simply sown directly in the ground. A third group of plants allows you to either direct sow (DS) or to start indoors (SI). In the north, starting indoors is the way to go. |
| Good Plants for Intensive Cultivation | These are fast-growing plants with shallow root systems that can be sown between rows of slow crops—arugula between broccoli plants, for example. |
| Can Be Sown 2 or 3 Times | These are plants that take a short time to mature and show good cold-hardiness. Three harvests will only happen in the south of Sweden. |
| Cold-Hardy To | The number indicates to how many degrees below freezing the plant will survive, in the best of circumstances. However, that doesn't mean the plant will grow simply because it has survived. Some plants can freeze and look terrible, only to perk up once temperatures rise. |
| Cut-and-Come-Again | A leafy plant that can be harvested over and over almost throughout the entire season. |
| Plant Family | The plant's botanical family. Good to know when you plan the crop rotation schedule. |

# CHEAT SHEET

| PLANT | COLD OR WARM WEATHER PLANT (C OR W) | PLANT SPACING | ROW SPACING | PLANTING DEPTH | LOWEST GERMINATION TEMPERATURE | DAYS TO GERMINA- TION | DAYS TO HARVEST |
|---|---|---|---|---|---|---|---|
| Red amaranth, et al. *Amaranthus cruentus* | W | 4"–6" (10 cm–15 cm) | 9 3/4"–11 3/4" (25 cm–30 cm) | 0.20" (0.5 cm) | 57.2°F (14°C) | 4–6 | 50–55 |
| Eggplant *Solanum melongena* | W | 19 1/2" x 19 1/2" (50 x 50 cm) | - | 0.20" (0.5 cm) | 68°F (20°C) | 10–20 | 140–200 |
| Mustard greens *Brassica juncea* | C | 6"–10" (15 cm–25 cm) | 12"–15 3/4" (30 cm–40 cm) | 1/3" (1 cm) | 41°F (5°C) | 5–8 | 40–50 |
| Celery, leaf *Apium graveolens* | C | 4"–6" (10 cm–15 cm) | 10"–12" (25 cm–30 cm) | 0–0.08" (0 cm–0.2 cm) | 64.4°F (18°C) | 14–21 | 80–110 |
| Celery, rib *Apium graveolens* | C | 12"–13 3/4" (30 cm–35 cm) | 15 3/4"–19 3/4" (40 cm–50 cm) | 0–0.08" | 18 | 14–21 | 180–240 |
| Cauliflower *Brassica oleracea* | C | 15 3/4"–17 3/4" (40 cm–45 cm) | 19 3/4"–23 1/2" (50 cm–60 cm) | 1/3" (1 cm) | 41°F (5°C) | 5–10 | 110–140 |
| Fava (broad) bean *Vicia faba* | C | 4"–6" (10 cm–15 cm) | 19 3/4"–23 1/2") (50 cm–60 cm) | 2"–2 3/4" (5 cm–7 cm) | 41°F (5°C) | 10–14 | 80–100 |
| Broccoli *Brassica oleracea* | C | 15 3/4"–19 3/4" (40 cm–50 cm) | 19 3/4"–23 1/2" (50 cm–60 cm) | 1/3" (1 cm) | 41°F (5°C) | 5–10 | 90–120 |
| Brussels sprouts *Brassica oleracea* | C | 19 3/4"–23 1/2" (50 cm–60 cm) | 23 1/2"–27 1/2" (60 cm–70 cm) | 1/3" (1 cm) | 41°F (5°C) | 5–10 | 190–210 |
| Green/snap/string bean *Phaseolus vulgaris* | W | 4"–4 3/4" (10 cm–12 cm) | 15 3/4"–19 3/4" (40 cm–50 cm) | 1 1/4" (3 cm) | 53.6°F (12°C) | 6–12 | 60–90 |
| Chili pepper/bell pepper *Capsicum annuum* et al. | W | 17 3/4" (45 cm) | 17 3/4"–19 3/4" (45 cm–50 cm) | 1/3" (1 cm) | 64.4°F (18°C) | 8–14 | 130–180 |
| Daikon and radish *Raphanus sativus* | C | 10" (25 cm) | 12"–13 3/4" (30 cm–35 cm) | 1/3" (1 cm) | 41°F (5°C) | 5–8 | 65–80 |
| Dill *Anethum graveolens* | C | 3/4"–2", 8" for flower (2 cm–5 cm, and 20 cm) | 12"–15 3/4" (30 cm–40 cm) | 1/3" (1 cm) | 41°F (5°C) | 12–15 | 30–60 |
| Frisée, escarole *Chicorium endiva* | C | 8 3/4"–13 3/4" (22 cm–30 cm) | 12"–13 3/4" (30 cm–35 cm) | 1/3" (1 cm) | 53.6°F (12°C) | 12–14 | 70–85 |
| Kale *Brassica oleracea* | C | 17 3/4"–21 1/2" (45 cm–55 cm) | 12"–113 3/4" (30 cm–35 cm) | 1/3" (1 cm) | 41°F (5°C) | 5–10 | 90–110 |
| Broccoli rabe *Brassica rapa* | C | 6"–9 3/4" (15 cm–25 cm) | 12"–13 3/4" (30 cm–35 cm) | 1/3" (1 cm) | 53.6°F (12°C) | 7–8 | 40–60 |

| START INDOORS (SI) OR DIRECT SOW (DS) | INTER-PLANTING (BETWEEN ROWS) | STAGGERED SOWING | COLD-HARDY TO | CUT-AND-COME-AGAIN | CROSS- OR SELF-POLLINATOR | PLANT FAMILY |
|---|---|---|---|---|---|---|
| SI/DS | NO | YES | 32°F (0°C) | YES | C | Amaranthus |
| SI | NO | NO | 32°F (0°C) | NO | C | Solanaceae |
| DS | YES | YES | 23°F–19.4°F (-5°C to–7°C) | NO | C | Brassicaceae |
| SI | NO | NO | 23°F–21.2°F (-5°C to–6°C) | YES | C | Umbelliferae |
| SI | NO | NO | 23°F–21.2°F (-5°C to–6°C) | NO | C | Umbelliferae |
| SI | NO | NO | 32°F (0°C) | NO | C | Brassicaceae |
| SI | NO | NO | 19.4°F–15.8 (-7°C to–9°C) | NO | S | Leguminosae |
| SI | NO | NO | 26.6°F–24.8°F (-3°C to–4°C) | NO | C | Brassicaceae |
| SI | NO | NO | 15.8°F–14°F (-9°C to–10°C) | NO | C | Brassicaceae |
| SI | NO | NO | 32°F (0°C) | NO | S | Leguminosae |
| SI | NO | NO | 32°F (0°C) | NO | S | Solanaceae |
| DS | NO | YES | 21.2°F–15.8°F | NO | C | Brassicaceae |
| SI | YES | YES | 28.4°F–24.8°F | NO | C | Umbelliferae |
| DS | NO | YES | 26.6°F–24.8°F (-3°C to–4°C) | NO | C | Asteraceae |
| SI/DS | NO | YES | 0.4°F (-18°C) | YES | C | Brassicaceae |
| DS | NO | NO | 26.6°F–24.8°F (-3°C to -4°C) | NO | C | Brassicaceae |

*cont. on next page*

cont. from previous page

| PLANT | COLD OR WARM WEATHER PLANT (C OR W) | PLANT SPACING | ROW SPACING | PLANTING DEPTH | LOWEST GERMINATION TEMPERATURE | DAYS TO GERMINA-TION | DAYS TO HARVEST |
|---|---|---|---|---|---|---|---|
| Cucumber *Cucumis sativus* | W | 6"–8" (15 cm–20 cm) | 39 1/2"–47 1/4" (100 cm–120 cm) | 3/4"–1 1/4" (2 cm–3 cm) | 59°F (15°C) | 6–9 | 60–75 |
| Jerusalem artichoke (tubers) *Helanthius tuberosus* | C | 12"–15 3/4" (30 cm–40 cm) | 31 1/2" (80 cm) | 4"–6" (10 cm –15 cm) | 41°F (5°C) | 14–28 | 140–180 |
| Chinese chives *Allium tuberosum* | C | 1/3"–3/4" (1 cm–2 cm) | 12"–15 3/4" (30 cm–40 cm) | 1/3" (1 cm) | 41°F (5°C) | 7–15 | 100–120 |
| Globe artichoke *Cynara scolymus* | W | 39 1/2" x 39 1/2" (100 cm x 100 cm) | - | 1/3" (1 cm) | 68°F (20°C) | 8–14 | 180–200 |
| Cabbage, white and red *Brassica oleracea* | C | 15 3/4"–21 1/2" (40 cm–55 cm) | 19 3/4"–27 1/2" (50 cm–70 cm) | 1/3" (1 cm) | 41°F (5°C) | 5–10 | 60–140 |
| Kohlrabi *Brassica oleracea* | C | 8"–10" (20 cm–25 cm) | 12"–15 3/4" (30 cm–40 cm) | 1/3" (1 cm) | 41°F (5°C) | 5–8 | 70–110 |
| Rutabaga *Brassica napus* | C | 12"–13 3/4" (30 cm–35 cm) | 19 3/4" (50 cm) | 1/3" (1 cm) | 41°F (5°C) | 5–8 | 85–90 |
| Onion (yellow and red onion sets) *Allium cepa* | C | 3 1/4"–4" (8 cm–10 cm) | 10"–12" (25 cm–30 cm) | 3/4"–1 1/4" (2 cm–3 cm) | 41°F (5°C) | 12–14 | 60–80 |
| Onion, from seed *Allium cepa* | C | 3 1/4"–4" (8 cm–10 cm) | 10"–12" (25 cm–30 cm) | 3/4" (2 cm) | 41°F (5°C) | 15–17 | 120–150 |
| Turnip *Brassica rapa* | C | 4"–6" (10 cm–15 cm) | 12"–15 3/4" (30 cm–40 cm) | 1/3" (1 cm) | 41°F (5°C) | 5–8 | 40–55 |
| Corn *Zea mays* | W | 10" (25 cm) | 27 1/2"–31 1/2" (70 cm–80 cm) | 1 1/4"–1 3/4" (3 cm–4 cm) | 59°F (15°C) | 10–12 | 120–140 |
| Malabar spinach *Basella rubra* | W | 10"–12" (25 cm–30 cm) | 12"–13 3/4" (30 cm–35 cm) | 1/3" (1 cm) | 68°F (20°C) | 14–21 | 90 -110 |
| Chard, spinach beet *Beta vulgaris* | C | 4"–6" (10 cm–15 cm) | 15 3/4" (40 cm) | 1/3"–3/4" (1 cm–2 cm) | 44.6°F (7°C) | 8–14 | 45–60 |
| Carrot *Daucus carota* | C | 1 1/2"–2 1/2" (4 cm–6 cm) | 10"–15 3/4" (25 cm–40 cm) | 1/3" (1 cm) | 42.8°F (6°C) | 10–17 | 90–140 |
| Melon *Cucumis melo* | W | 15 3/4"–23 1/2" (40 cm–60 cm) | 23 1/2" (60 cm) | 3/4"–1 1/4" (2 cm–3 cm) | 68°F–71.6°F (20°C–22°C) | 7–10 | 95–105 |
| Mizuna cabbage *Brassica rapa* | C | 8"–13 3/4" (20 cm–35 cm) | 12"–15 3/4" (30 cm–40 cm) | 1/3" (1 cm) | 41°F (5°C) | 5–8 | 40–50 |
| New Zealand spinach *Tetragonia tetragonoides* | W | 17 3/4" x 17 3/4" (45 cm x 45 cm) | 10"–12" (25 cm–30 cm) | 3/4"–1 1/4" (2 cm–3 cm) | 59°F (15°C) | 14–21 | 75–85 |

| START INDOORS (SI) OR DIRECT SOW (DS) | INTER-PLANTING (BETWEEN ROWS) | STAGGERED SOWING | COLD-HARDY TO | CUT-AND-COME-AGAIN | CROSS- OR SELF-POLLINATOR | PLANT FAMILY |
|---|---|---|---|---|---|---|
| SI/DS | NO | NO | 32°F (0°C) | NO | C | Cucurbitaceae |
| D | NO | NO | 16–20 | NO | C | Asteraceae |
| SI/DS | NO | NO | 26.6°F–23°F (-3°C to -5°C) | YES | C | Alliaceae |
| SI | NO | NO | 32°F (0°C) | NO | S | Asteraceae |
| SI | NO | NO | 24.8°F–21.2°F (-4°C to –6°C) | NO | C | Brassicaceae |
| DS | NO | YES | 19.4°F–15.8°F (-7°C to -9°C) | NO | C | Brassicaceae |
| DS | NO | NO | 14°F–10.4°F (-10°C to -12°C) | NO | C | Brassicaceae |
| DS | YES | YES | 6.8°F–0.4°F (-14°C to -18°C) | NO | C | Alliaceae |
| SI/DS | NO | NO | 6.8°F–0.4°F (-14°C to -18°C) | NO | C | Alliaceae |
| DS | YES | YES | 23°F–21.2°F (-5°C to -6°C) | NO | C | Brassicaceae |
| SI | NO | NO | 32°F (0°C) | NO | C | Poaceae |
| SI | NO | NO | 32°F (0°C) | YES | S | Basellaceae |
| DS | NO | YES | YES 15.8°F–10.4°F (-9°C to -12°C) | YES | C | Amaranthus |
| DS | NO | YES (early varieties) | 15.8°F–12.2°F (-9°C to -11°C) | NO | C | Umbelliferae |
| SI | NO | NO | 32°F (0°C) | NO | C | Cucurbitaceae |
| DS | NO | YES | 24.8°F–21.2°F (-4°C to -6°C) | YES | C | Brassicaceae |
| SI | NO | NO | 32°F (0°C) | YES | S | Asteraceae |

*cont. on next page*

*cont. from previous page*

| PLANT | COLD OR WARM WEATHER PLANT (C OR W) | PLANT SPACING | ROW SPACING | PLANTING DEPTH | LOWEST GERMINATION TEMPERATURE | DAYS TO GERMINA-TION | DAYS TO HARVEST |
|---|---|---|---|---|---|---|---|
| Lacinato (Tuscan) kale<br>*Brassica oleracea* | C | 17³/₄"–21¹/₂" (45 cm–55 cm) | 19³/₄"–23¹/₂" (50 cm–60 cm) | ¹/₃" (1 cm) | 41°F (5°C) | 5–10 | 90–110 |
| Parsley<br>*Petroselinum crispum* | C | 2"–3¹/₂" (5 cm–8 cm) | 13³/₄"–10" (25 cm–35 cm) | 0.19" (0.5 cm) | 41°F (5°C) | 14–21 | 75–85 |
| Potato (seed potato)<br>*Solanum tuberosum* | C | 8"–11³/₄" (5 cm–8 cm) | 23¹/₂"–27¹/₂" (60 cm–70 cm) | 2³/₄"–4" (7 cm–10 cm) | 41°F (5°C) | 10–14 | 90–130 |
| Pumpkin and squash<br>*Cucurbita pepo, C. maxima* | W | 39¹/₂" (100 cm) | 39¹/₂" (100 cm) | ³/₄"–1¹/₄" (2 cm–3 cm) | 62.6°F (17°C) | 6–10 | 90–140 |
| Leek<br>*Allium porrum* | C | 6"–8" (15 cm–20 cm) | 15³/₄"–19³/₄" (40 cm–50 cm) | ¹/₃" (1 cm) | 39.2°F (4°C) | 7–15 | 160–200 |
| Scarlet runner bean<br>*Phaseolus coccineus* | W | 4"–4³/₄" (10 cm–12 cm) | 15³/₄"–19³/₄" (40 cm–50 cm) | 1¹/₄"–2" (3 cm–5 cm) | 53.6°F (12°C) | 8–12 | 70–90 |
| Celeriac<br>*Aplum graveolens* | C | 11³/₄" (30 cm) | 19³/₄" (50 cm) | 0.078" (0–0.2 cm) | 64.4°F (18°C) | 14–21 | 180–220 |
| Parsley root<br>*Petroselinum crispum* | C | 4" (10 cm) | 12" (30 cm) | ¹/₃" (1 cm) | 41°F (5°C) | 14–21 | 100-110 |
| Arugula, rocket<br>*Eruca sativa* | C | 1¹/₂"–4" (4 cm–10 cm) | 8"–12" (20 cm–30 cm) | ¹/₃" (1 cm) | 41°F (5°C) | 5–7 | 25–30 |
| Radish<br>*Raphanus sativus* | C | ³/₄"–1¹/₄" (2 cm–3 cm) | 4"–8" (10 cm–20 cm) | ¹/₃" (1 cm) | 41°F (5°C) | 5–10 | 25–35 |
| Beetroot<br>*Beta vulgaris* | C | 2"–4" (5 cm–10 cm) | 12"–15³/₄" (30 cm–40 cm) | ¹/₃"–³/₄" (1 cm–2 cm) | 44.6°F (7°C) | 8–14 | 55–75 |
| Scallions<br>*Allium cepa* | C | ³/₄" (2 cm) | 12" (30 cm) | ¹/₃" (1 cm) | 39.2°F (4°C) | 7–15 | 70-100 |
| Napa cabbage<br>*Brassica rapa* | C | 10"–13³/₄" (25 cm–35 cm) | 15³/₄"–17³/₄" (40 cm–45 cm) | ¹/₃" (1 cm) | 59°F (15°C) | 5–8 | 60–70 |
| Lettuce (romaine, leaf, head, batavia)<br>*Lactuca sativa* | C | 8"–12" (20 cm–30 cm) | 12"–15¹/₄" (30 cm–40 cm) | ¹/₃" (1 cm) | 41°F (5°C) | 7–10 | 50–70 |
| Curly endive, frisée<br>*Cichorium intybus* | C | 10"–13³/₄" (25 cm–35 cm) | 15³/₄"–19³/₄" (40 cm–50 cm) | ¹/₃" (1 cm) | 53.6°F (12°C) | 12–14 | 80–100 |
| Savoy cabbage<br>*Brassica oleracea* | C | 12"–15³/₄" (30 cm–40 cm) | 19³/₄"–23¹/₂" (50 cm–60 cm) | ¹/₃" (1 cm) | 41°F (5°C) | 5–10 | 90–140 |
| Kale, Red Russian<br>*Brassica napus* | C | 15³/₄"–17³/₄" (40 cm–45 cm) | 19³/₄"–23¹/₂" (50 cm–60 cm) | ¹/₃" (1 cm) | 41°F (5°C) | 5–8 | 50–60 |

| START INDOORS (SI) OR DIRECT SOW (DS) | INTER-PLANTING (BETWEEN ROWS) | STAGGERED SOWING | COLD-HARDY TO | CUT-AND-COME-AGAIN | CROSS- OR SELF-POLLINATOR | PLANT FAMILY |
|---|---|---|---|---|---|---|
| SI/DS | NO | YES | 17.6°F (-8°C) | YES | C | Brassicaceae |
| DS | NO | NO | 17.6°F–14°F (-8°C to -10°C) | YES | C | Umbelliferae |
| SI | NO | NO | 32°F (0°C) | NO | - | Solanaceae |
| SI | NO | NO | 32°F (0°C) | NO | C | Cucurbitaceae |
| SI | NO | NO | 17.6°F–10.4°F (-8°C–to -12°C) | NO | C | Alliaceae |
| SI/DS | NO | NO | 32°F (0°C) | NO | S | Leguminosae |
| SI | NO | NO | 21.2°F–19.4°F (-6°C to -7°C) | NO | S | Umbelliferae |
| DS | NO | NO | 19.4°F–15.8°F (−7°C to -9°C) | NO | C | Umbelliferae |
| DS | YES | YES | 23°F–21.2°F (-5°C to -6°C) | NO | C | Brassicaceae |
| DS | YES | YES | 21.2°F–17.6°F (-6°C to -8°C) | NO | C | Brassicaceae |
| DS | NO | YES (early varieties) | 21.2°F–17.6°F (-6°C to -8°C) | NO | C | Amaranthus |
| SI/DS | NO | NO | 24.8°F–0.4°F (-4°C to -18°C) | YES | C | Alliaceae |
| SI/DS | NO | NO | 26.6°F–23°F (-3°C to -5°C) | NO | C | Brassicaceae |
| DS | YES | YES | 26.6°F–23°F (-3°C to -5°C) | YES (leaf) | S | Asteraceae |
| SI/DS | NO | NO | 24.8°F–14°F (-4°C to -10°C) | NO | C | Asteraceae |
| SI | NO | NO | 14°F (-10°C) | NO | C | Brassicaceae |
| SI/DS | NO | YES | 17.6°F–14°F (-8°C to -10°C) | YES | C | Brassicaceae |

*cont. on next page*

| PLANT | COLD OR WARM WEATHER PLANT (C OR W) | PLANT SPACING | ROW SPACING | PLANTING DEPTH | LOWEST GERMINATION TEMPERATURE | DAYS TO GERMINA- TION | DAYS TO HARVEST |
|---|---|---|---|---|---|---|---|
| Garden cress *Lepidium sativum var. crispum* | C | 1¼"–2" (3 cm–5 cm) | 6" (15 cm) | ⅓" (1 cm) | 41°F (5°C) | 3–5 | 21–28 |
| Eurpean barilla plant *Salsola soda* | C | 6"–8" (15 cm–20 cm) | 10"–12" (25 cm–30 cm) | ⅓" (1 cm) | 60.8°F (16°C) | 8–12 | 60–80 |
| Spinach *Spinacia oleracea* | C | 2"–4" (5 cm–10 cm) | 12"–15¾" (30 cm–40 cm) | ⅓"–¾" (1 cm–2 cm) | 41°F (5°C) | 5–10 | 35–45 |
| Sweetheart (pointy cabbage) *Brassica oleracea* | C | 12"–15¾" (30 cm–40 cm) | 15¾"–19½" (40 cm–50 cm) | ⅓" (1 cm) | 41°F (5°C) | 5–10 | 60–80 |
| Minutina (Erba Stella) *Plantago coronopus* | C | 4" (10 cm) | 12" (30 cm) | 0–0.08" (0 cm–0.2 cm) | 41°F (5°C) | 7–10 | 30–50 |
| Salsify *Scorzonera hispanica* | C | 4"–6" (10 cm–15 cm) | 15¾" (40 cm) | ⅓" (1 cm) | 41°F (5°C) | 10–12 | 120–150 |
| Sweet fennel *Foeniculum vulgare* | W | 8" (20 cm) | 15¾"–19¾" (40 cm–50 cm) | ⅓" (1 cm) | 50°F (10°C) | 14–21 | 100–110 |
| Tomato *Solanum lycopesicum* | W | 17¾"–21¾" (45 cm–55 cm) | 23½"–27½" (60 cm–70 cm) | ⅓" (1 cm) | 57.2°F (14°C) | 6–10 | 110–160 |
| Mountain spinach or orache *Atriplex hortensis* | C | 10"–11¾" (25 cm–30 cm) | 11¾"–13¾" (30 cm–35 cm) | ⅓"–¾" (1 cm–¾ cm) | 50°F (10°C) | 7–15 | 50–60 |
| Common purslane *Portulaca oleracea* | W | 4"–6" (10 cm–15 cm) | 10"–11¾" (25 cm–30 cm) | ⅓" (1 cm) | 53.6°F (12°C) | 14–21 | 50–60 |
| Watercress *Nasturtium officinale* | C | 4" (10 cm) | 6" (15 cm) | 0.19" (0,5 cm) | 41°F (5°C) | 10–20 | 60–80 |
| Winter purslane or Miner's lettuce *Claytonia perfoliata* | C | 2" (5 cm) | 8" (20 cm) | 0.19" (0.5 cm) | 41°F (5°C) | 7–15 | 40–60 |
| Mâche, Lamb's lettuce *Valerianella locusta* | C | 2" (5 cm) | 8" (20 cm) | ⅓" (1 cm) | 41°F (5°C) | 5–10 | 55–85 |
| Land or American cress *Barbarea verna* | C | 6" (15 cm) | 8"–10" (20 cm–25 cm) | ⅓" (1 cm) | 41°F (5°C) | 5–15 | 40–50 |
| Garlic (cloves) *Allium sativum* | C | 6" (15 cm) | 8"–13¾" (20 cm–35 cm) | 2½" (6 cm) | Plant in fall | - | 280–320 |
| Green peas *Pisum Sativum* | C | 2½"–3" | 12"–17¾" (30 cm–45 cm) | 1¼" (3 cm) | 41°F (5°C) dwarf peas 50°F (10°C) | 6–12 | 50–70 |

| START INDOORS (SI) OR DIRECT SOW (DS) | INTER-PLANTING (BETWEEN ROWS) | STAGGERED SOWING | COLD-HARDY TO | CUT-AND-COME-AGAIN | CROSS- OR SELF-POLLINATOR | PLANT FAMILY |
|---|---|---|---|---|---|---|
| DS | YES | YES | 26.6°F–24.8°F (-3°C to -4°C) | NO | C | Asteraceae |
| SI | NO | NO | 32°F (0°C) | YES | C | Amaranthus |
| DS | YES | YES | 21.2°F–17.6°F (-6°C to–8°C) | NO | C | Amaranthus |
| SI | NO | NO | 24.8°F–21.2°F (-4°C to -6°C) | NO | C | Brassicaceae |
| SI/DS | NO | NO | 6.8°F–0.4°F (-14°C to -18°C) | YES | C | Plantaginaceae |
| DS | NO | NO | 3.2°F–0.4°F (-16°C to -18°C) | NO | C | Asteraceae |
| SI/DS | NO | NO | 26.6°F–23°F (-3°C to -5°C) | NO | C | Umbelliferae |
| SI | NO | NO | 32°F (0°C) | NO | C | Solanaceae |
| DS | NO | YES | 28.4°F–26.6°F (-2°C to -3°C) | YES | C | Amaranthus |
| DS | NO | YES | 32°F (0°C) | YES | C | Portulacaceae |
| SI/DS | NO | NO | 26.6°F–21.2°F (-3°C to -6°C) | YES | C | Brassicaceae |
| DS | NO | YES | 3.2°F–0.4°F (-16°C to–18°C) | YES | C | Portulacaceae |
| DS | NO | NO | 3.2°F–0.4°F (-16°C to -18°C) | YES | C | Valerianaceae |
| SI/DS | NO | NO | 17.6°F–14°F (-8°C to–10°C) | YES | C | Brassicaceae |
| DS | NO | NO | 3.2°F–0.4°F (-16°C to -18°C) | NO | - | Alliaceae |
| DS | NO | NO | 26.6°F–23°F (-3°C to -5°C) | NO | S | Leguminosae |

*Pages 20–21: These are all cold weather crops: Batavia lettuce, curly garden cress, chard, and parsley.*
*Pages 26–27: Pumpkins and squash from the world over—these are all warm weather plants.*

**25**

# CREATE A GREENHOUSE ENVIRONMENT

**PLASTIC AND GLASS MAKE IT POSSIBLE TO HARVEST PRODUCE AS SOON AS THE COLTSFOOT IS IN FLOWER, AND UNTIL THE TREES SHED THEIR LEAVES. CANDY CONTAINERS, WOVEN ROW FABRIC, AND TUNNELS HELP CREATE A GREENHOUSE ENVIRONMENT.**

COMMUNITY GARDEN GROWERS have always been very smart about creating greenhouse environments without using actual greenhouses. My favorite method is using plastic candy containers that I get for free at the grocery store. I discovered this many years ago on a visit to the Alby community gardens outside Stockholm. An elderly gentleman stood amid a forest of ski poles, which he used to stake his tomato plants. Lettuces were covered with plastic candy containers into which he had punched air holes. This was his greenhouse setup.

Since then I have also used candy containers as mini greenhouses, and as shields against slugs. Another way is to use PET (recyclable) plastic bottles with the bottoms cut out and a screw-on cap.

## GARDEN FABRIC IS A MUST

However, the most important tool is not plastic boxes but garden fabric, also called row covers. I'm adamant about using this fabric: It must be put down in spring and early summer, and preferably in late fall, too. It gets 2 to 3 degrees warmer under the cover, the temperature remains steady, and the soil doesn't dry out so quickly, which in turn helps seeds germinate faster and grow stronger. Yields are higher overall, but primarily there's the flavor—wow, such flavors! Turnips and radishes grown under row covers are gourmet-grade compared to those grown uncovered.

I usually set the covers down at the time of planting. And when are they removed? Well, when you stand in front of the plants and can happily exclaim: "They grow like weeds!" You can leave the covers on longer, but it isn't necessary. In my area, it means that I remove the fabric sometime around the beginning or middle of June.

You can put covers down a week or two before planting, if you prefer. It warms up the soil. Translucent or black plastic sheeting works, too.

The covers become useful again in the fall—outdoors, in greenhouses, and in growing tunnels. You'll raise the temperature by a few degrees if you combine an unheated tunnel with

*All the ways that replicate a greenhouse environment are good; for example, PET (recyclable) plastic bottles with the bottoms cut out.*

row covers. But we'll circle back to this topic in the chapter about fall.

There are some drawbacks to garden fabric. It's ugly and awkward to handle. A lot of stones and wooden planks are required to secure the material to the ground. And if that weren't enough, weeds thrive underneath it, and sometimes slugs do, too. That's why I sometimes lift the covers to weed and hunt for slugs.

About thirty years ago, when I first started using garden fabric, I used to wash it once or twice in the washing machine. But the quality of today's fabric is not the same, and it would probably not survive a single wash. These days I put the fabric out the second year, unwashed, hoping the rain will rinse it clean while saying a little prayer that it will not tear. Occasionally my prayer is answered.

The fabric also helps protect against insect infestations, especially from the carrot, onion, and cabbage flies and cabbage moths. But that means that the cover must be left on the entire season, and that there are no gaps between the fabric and the soil. By the way, the fabric also protects against problem birds.

### GARDEN FABRIC FACTS
• Row covers are made from pressed polypropylene fibers. They let through water and about 80 to 90 percent of the light. The fabric is usually somewhat UV-resistant.

• The most common fabrics weigh around 0.59 oz. per 10 ¾ sq. ft. (17 grams per square meter). Go for 0.67 oz. per sq. ft. (19 grams per square meter), as it will hold up better to wear and tear. It will let in a little less light, but the difference is negligible.

• The covers should lay loosely over the plants and be roomy enough so that you can anchor it along all the sides. Approximately 8' (240 cm) is usually enough for a garden bed that measures about 4' to 4 ¼' (120 to 130 cm). This works also for pallet rims.

*Garden fabric can be draped and attached over bendable PVC pipes.*

*Cold frames made from recycled plastic windows*

• Tall plants can get damaged if they're covered when it's windy, so it's best to place the fabric over support hoops or something similar. There are premade hoops for pallet rims available in stores.

• Another option is to use a PVC pipe that you can easily bend into a hoop.

### GROWING IN A COLD FRAME
A cold frame is an itty-bitty greenhouse. It consists of a wooden frame that's approximately 1' to 1 ¼' (25 to 40 cm) high, with a hinged window

**30**

## HOW TO BUILD A COLD FRAME

A classic cold frame model: a south-leaning frame covered by a window.

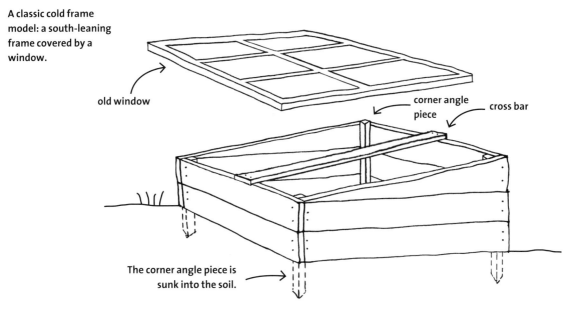

old window

corner angle piece

cross bar

The corner angle piece is sunk into the soil.

that opens. It heats up under the glass, which allows growing to start earlier in the season. It can also go on longer into fall.

Today there are premade cold frames you can buy, but it's easy to build your own—you can refer to the instructions at the top of this page. If you can't find any old windows, make your own by nailing together wooden slats and then tightening some poly sheeting over them. There are premade windows available in stores if you grow plants in a pallet rim.

Fill the cold frame with 6" to 8" (15 to 20 cm) of loose, nutrient-rich soil, preferably amended with compost. Now you just have to sow or plant. However, don't forget that the frame needs to be aired out every day. You can place a wooden wedge between the main frame and the window, for example.

The warmer the weather, the more you'll need to air the frame out. If it's sweltering outside, remove the window altogether, or open it up wide. The maximum temperature inside the frame should not exceed 77°F to 86°F (25°C to 30°C).

I use my cold frame to force plants. A few rows of extremely early lettuce also have dedicated row space. In late summer, I let my watercress spread. Maybe you have some other favorite plant you'd like to keep warm and protect from the wind. Why not choose melons, which were once commonly grown in cold frames, or cucumbers?

A cold frame can also be used as a warm frame. Stable-animal manure is the only missing thing. Read more about warm frames on p. 126.

### BUILD A COLD FRAME

**1. Choose a sunny site.** Gather some old windows (check with demolition companies or online).

**2. Build the frame** using planks (not pressure-treated or covered in weatherproofing chemicals) to a height of 1' to 1 ¼' (25 to 40 cm). Adjust the other measurements to fit the windows. To ensure that the windows stay firmly in place, put crossbars across the frame. Position the windows on the crossbars.

**3. Wedge angle pieces** inside the frame's corners, screwing or nailing them on. Lean the frame

*My own cold frame with glass windows. Watercress grows there in the fall.*

*Middle Eastern community gardeners build this type of cold frame in rows.*

slightly toward the south, either by placing the frame on a slope or by building it with the front 2" to 4" (5 to 10 cm) lower than the back. Treat the wood with linseed oil.

## GARDENING IN A GREENHOUSE TUNNEL

My own tunnel adventure began when I met some very skilled Chinese growers. They grew water spinach in 3¼' (1 meter) high plastic tunnels. This was a plant I yearned for but had had no success in growing. There just isn't a crisper stir-fried vegetable out there.

The plastic was fastened over beautifully woven hoops made from tree branches found in the woods. It's hard to picture that a plastic contraption in the community garden could be so beautiful. Inside those hoops, watercress flourished.

I went home and started planning my own tunnel. Sadly, I wasn't able to weave a hoop; I had to use PVC piping instead; it is pliable so it can be bent into hoops very easily.

Now even I can grow water spinach, as well as chili and bell peppers, eggplant and bush tomatoes—at least when we have decent summers.

Now and then I roll up the plastic on one side to check that everything is going according to plan. The following are instructions on how to build your own greenhouse tunnel.

### BUILDING A LOW GREENHOUSE TUNNEL

1. **Prepare a garden bed with good soil** and edge it with wooden planks. A suitable bed width is 4' to 4¼' (120 to 130 cm), but it can be as long as you wish. When you decide on the height you want, remember that the plastic should not lay on the plants. Usually, 3¼' (1 meter) is enough.

2. **Screw down pipe clamps** along the edging's long sides, spacing them 2' (60 cm) apart. This is where you anchor the hoops. Push down the PVC pipes so they form hoops across the bed. Once all the hoops are inserted, place a pipe

**32**

*My movable growing tunnel is made with strong wooden slats, PVC pipes, and greenhouse plastic.*

across the top of the hoops and fasten it at each point where it intersects with the hoops. This will make the tunnel rigid and stable.

**3. Cover the greenhouse** with greenhouse or reinforced poly sheeting. Attach the plastic to the hoops with clamps; in addition to being really efficient, they are easily available at your local home improvement store. You need to leave a generous 3 ¼' (1 meter) of extra plastic at the openings. That way you can close the openings by clamping the plastic together. Leave them open during the height of summer.

**4. A moveable tunnel** is a cool hack. You can shift the tunnel around as you wish during the season, setting it where you think the plants will get extra warmth and protection from the wind. Instead of affixing the hoops to the edging planks, build a frame out of, say, sturdy wooden slats measuring 1 ¾" × 3 ¾" (45 × 94 mm), and fasten the hoops to the frame.

## UNHEATED GREENHOUSES AND TUNNEL (POLY-TUNNEL) GREENHOUSES

Next in my exploration of tunnels was to figure out a reasonable solution for the high, indeterminate tomato plants that grow too big for low tunnels. Growing tomatoes outdoors is not ideal because summer is both too cool and too short. And if that weren't enough, an even bigger headache has flared up in the guise of "potato late blight fungus," also known simply as "late blight." In worst-case scenarios, it can strike as early as in July. (Read more about tomatoes and late blight on p. 88).

I've found a solution to this problem that I'm absolutely delighted with, and it's the tunnel greenhouse; it provides tomatoes with a certain degree of protection against fungal attacks. Also, tomatoes ripen more quickly, which means that mold spores don't get the opportunity to damage quite so much of the harvest.

But a tunnel greenhouse has much more to offer. I can grow exactly what I want, and I always end up with better yields than from anything planted outside in unprotected beds. The conditions for a record-long growing season are optimal.

A tunnel greenhouse has a frame made of galvanized steel pipes wrapped in a form-fitted polyethylene film. It may sound flimsy, but if the frame is adequately anchored, the construction can withstand surprisingly strong winds.

You can choose to leave the film on year-round, or you can remove it during the winter. The second option is best for us growers in community gardens, because for whatever reason, some community garden associations will only allow greenhouses on the allotments if the cover is taken off before winter. Why? Your guess is as good as mine!

A tunnel greenhouse is much more affordable than a traditional greenhouse, so you can opt to set up a larger structure. The bigger the space, the happier your plants will be. Another advantage of a greenhouse tunnel is that it's easier to assemble than a traditional greenhouse.

*Happiness: freshly harvested warm weather produce.*

But since both types of greenhouses operate the same way, my advice applies to both greenhouse tunnels and unheated, traditional greenhouses.

### GO FOR HEAT SEEKERS

So, what are you going to grow in your greenhouse? My suggestion is to choose plants that love heat, those that won't thrive if planted outside and unprotected. It seems a bit pointless to save the greenhouse tunnel for kale, when kale does just fine in the ground outside. That said, in early spring and late fall even kale will require a bit of cover. This is more or less how I divvy up the space inside my greenhouse tunnel:

**In spring:** early, fast-growing and cold-hardy greens, radishes and turnips.

**In summer:** warm weather plants such as tomatoes, cucumbers, bell peppers, eggplants, and chili peppers. I let them take up most of the space.

**In fall:** when tomato and cucumber plants are discarded, hopefully I have a few plants such as Asian leafy greens, kale, lettuce, and chard ready to go; if that's the case, I'll plant them in top-dressed soil. I can harvest these plants well into late fall. I will also add row covers, which help raise the inside temperature further.

**In winter:** over-wintering of fall plants.

Some prefer to grow a little of everything in their greenhouse, a bit like in a garden bed. That works too, of course. If you have trouble getting two or three harvests from your unprotected beds, a greenhouse will increase your chances of success. Don't forget that you can also force plants continuously for later needs—you collect the plants and use them to fill bare spots in the beds or in the greenhouse tunnel.

The advice I shared earlier (on p. 14) applies even to growing plants in a greenhouse. The main difference is that you can begin earlier, grow them over a longer period of time, and see vigorous growth in a greenhouse. In the chapters covering the seasons, you'll see recommendations on how to use the greenhouse at different times of the year. As usual, the cheat sheet is invaluable. With it, you'll be able to plan your cultivation.

### SOME FACTS ABOUT GREENHOUSE TUNNELS

**Where do you buy greenhouse tunnels?** First and foremost, look online. Make sure to get clear and detailed instructions on how to set up the tunnel, and check for a customer service number you can call if you need assistance. In the industry, tunnel greenhouses are also referred to as poly-tunnels or hoop-houses.

**What size?** The bigger the better. From a growing standpoint, 54 square feet (5 square meters) is pretty small; it's better to add some square footage. Its height should be at least 6 ½ feet (2 meters). A big greenhouse tunnel is also easier to maintain.

**What type of greenhouse plastic should I use?** Polyethylene plastic is best—even from an environmental perspective—and there needs to be UV protection. You'll find poly-tunnels available for sale that are made either of reinforced green plastic, or of translucent nonreinforced plastic. The variation in light conductivity is minimal, since both let in about 95 to 98 percent of the light, which is plenty. As of yet, there is no research into the difference in the quality of both materials, but there are reports that the green plastic might lead to plants growing more lanky and spindly. The framework should always be made of galvanized steel tubes; the thicker the tubes, the better.

**Can poly-tunnels withstand strong winds?** You might be better off with a traditional greenhouse if you live in an extremely windy location. I have seen some reports about plastic getting shredded in stormy weather in a few open locations.

**What are the ventilation requirements?** There must be vents or flaps on both sides of the tunnel, and preferably a door at each short end.

**Placement?** A north-south orientation is the common suggestion for a stationary greenhouse, but east-west works fine, too. The most important thing is to situate the greenhouse where it won't be in the shade. You'll need to give this proper consideration if you'll be placing it where there are trees nearby. A greenhouse needs to be outside of the tree canopy's edge plus an additional 6 ½ feet (2 meters), or you'll soon discover tree roots in your plantings. It's always to your advantage to set the greenhouse so the wind hits its long side, which can withstand stronger winds than the short sides. Make sure that you plan for proper walkways around the greenhouse, measuring at least 2 ¼' (70 cm) or wider.

**What happens if the plastic shreds?** Damage can be fixed with duct tape or special tape sold by the greenhouse manufacturer. Tape won't work for splicing; it's better to use clamps.

**Will I need a building permit?** Sometimes, you can set up a greenhouse tunnel without a building permit if you remove the plastic during winter. However, check with your city planning office to be on the safe side.

**How are poly-tunnels secured in the ground?** There are many different ways to secure the frame to the ground—using anchor plates, for example. The greenhouse manufacturer can usually provide good advice here.

The plastic overlaps by just over 1 ½' (50 cm) at the bottom, which makes it possible to anchor it by digging a trench and covering the plastic with soil. Instead of using soil, you can also plant beds all around the outside perimeter of the greenhouse. This is not practical if you're going to take the plastic off the frame for the winter, in which case you'll need to secure the plastic with stones, flag stones, or sand bags. Don't forget that the plastic must be stretched tightly over the frame, as this will reduce the risk of storm damage.

**Can it get too hot?** If it's 86°F (30°C) outside, it will be 104°F (40°C) inside the greenhouse. That is too warm for plants. They won't die or droop, but their ability to bear fruit will be impaired. This is true for tomatoes and bell peppers, for instance. Another negative side effect is that the tomatoes will not turn red; it could take forever for them to show any color at all. In this case you'll need to use shade fabric.

This page shows a 126.18 sq. ft. (12 square meter) tunnel greenhouse; to the right is a poly-tunnel built with PVC pipes and plastic construction sheeting.

# THE FERTILE EARTH

**ENGAGING IN INTENSIVE CULTIVATION MAKES A LOT OF DEMANDS ON THE SOIL. YOU'RE USING THE SAME DIRT AS A TRADITIONAL GARDENER, BUT THE GROWING SEASON IS TWICE AS LONG. THIS MEANS THAT YOUR SOIL MUST BE IN TOP CONDITION.**

IT'S AN AMAZING ADVENTURE, as wonderful as gardening itself, to witness once totally barren earth turn into black, fertile soil. But it doesn't happen overnight, even if you do notice positive changes as early as in your first season. Also, keep in mind that no one has this type of soil handed to them on a platter. At least I've never heard this happening to anyone.

All soils need to be amended, whether they're hardpan clay or thin, sandy soil. This you'll do chiefly by increasing the soil's humus content, which is something that all soils lack. Once that's done, you'll have more nutrient-rich and airy soil, and in the bargain, a swarm of beneficial microorganisms.

## HEAVENLY HUMUS

Humus is organic matter found in, among other things, composted soil, grass clippings, leaves, pulled weeds, and manure (from both cows and horses). Peat also contains humus, but it's quickly broken down and totally lacking in microorganisms and nutrients. It can, however, be used in a pinch.

Composting, mulching, and fertilizing with manure—all three of these methods contribute to a boost in humus content.

In two or three years' time the soil will be dark brown and friable, and you will have reached your goal. The mineral particles stick together to form tiny little compounds called aggregates, not unlike breadcrumbs. This is what makes the soil porous.

However, you must continue to amend the soil by adding organic matter each year, or else the amount of humus within the soil will dwindle again. But at this point you don't need to use as much organic matter as when you began building up the soil at the start.

You don't have to worry about the soil's pH value once you've reached a high level of humus, because it self-regulates in a humus-rich environment. Only if the growth is puny and you live in an area with consistently low pH values might it be a good idea to test the soil.

On the next page, I've gathered some basic information about vegetable gardening. It's not a bad idea to take a look at it before bringing out your spade.

*Left: Not too little and not too much fertilizer makes for great-looking and tasty beets.*

## IMPORTANT TO KNOW WHEN GROWING VEGETABLES

Vegetables require *at least seven hours of full sun every day.* Only kale, arugula, leaf lettuce, chard, and other leafy greens can handle part shade.

**Soil depth** needs to be at least 15 ¾" (40 cm) or more; you can grow anything you like if you have that. For leafy greens, radishes, early beets, and other plants with shallow root systems, you can make do with only 8".

**A good microclimate** has significant effects on the result. If the area is windy, put up some wind barriers using fences, planks, or bushes. Make sure they don't cast shade on the plants.

**Drainage** must be effective or you'll have to reroute any water runoff, or find another planting site.

**Garden in raised beds** measuring 4" to 8" in height or more. Raised beds warm quickly in the spring and hold deeper amounts soil. A pallet rim is also

*I found these raised beds full of fertile soil in Gällivare, northern Sweden. Go Lapland, go!*

a raised bed; two rims on top of each other provide the perfect depth.

It's handy to set up *four beds* to create the ideal conditions for a four-year crop rotation (see p. 57). The paths between beds should measure about the width of a garden rake, or else it will be too difficult to maintain the beds.

Opt for large containers *if you garden on a balcony* or a deck; use tubs, boxes, barrels, and buckets that all have drainage holes at the bottom. Tomatoes and chili peppers thrive in buckets—one plant per bucket. You'll need a container with a large surface area for leafy greens such as lettuce and parsley. However, you won't need to plant them in deep soil, so a washtub will do fine.

**Potting soil** can be used if you don't have your own soil. Things will grow well, but they'll fare even better if you mix the potting soil with some added compost or garden soil. This will prevent the dirt from drying out too quickly, and you'll also introduce some microorganisms to it.

## TO DIG OR NOT TO DIG?

Traditionally, garden soil is dug in the fall. This is done so that the dirt clods can break apart into friable soil when the ground shifts as it thaws. The purpose is to have fine soil structure in the spring when it is time to sow.

But how does this square up with the organic grower's goal to create living soil rich in microbial life? Not very well. It's an undeniable fact that we disturb microorganisms when we dig. But if you won't dig, you run the risk of having soil that's impossible to work with come springtime.

Why not try to develop soil that is so porous that no digging is required? Such soils do exist. Year after year, this is dirt that's been mulched with straw, hay, grass clippings, and the like. Under this layer, worms and other organisms have created soil so airy that you can put away your spade.

*A leek bed mulched with fresh grass clippings, which fertilize and increase the humus content.*

Before you get to this point: Dig a clay soil in the fall! However, you don't have to turn the soil. Instead, push the spade into the soil and tip it backwards to loosen the clumps from the base. That's all you need to do, and it is kind to both the soil's microorganisms and your back. Easily worked soil can be dug in the spring.

By the way, do you realize how incredibly useful those microorganisms are? Soil without microbial life is like a restaurant without cooks. It's the microorganisms that bring and serve nutrients to our plants. A teaspoon of healthy soil can contain as many as one billion microorganisms and small insects; bacteria, fungi, millipedes, amoebae … not to mention the worms that turn leaves to nutrient-rich loam and whose burrowing through meandering tunnels loosen the dirt. And, last but not least, we have the mycorrhizal fungi, which live in symbiosis with the plants' roots and help them take up water and nutrients. They also protect against disease.

## MULCHING IS BEST

Mulching is the greatest way to improve the soil. There is nothing more natural than soil covered in organic matter. Just take a walk in the woods and check it out; here, everything is covered in organic matter that's more or less in a state of decomposition. That's where the plants get their nutrients.

Simply mulch the soil with organic waste and trimmings from your garden if you want rich and fertile dirt. The mulch will break down into great humus, and the soil will be crawling with worms. Cover with the soil with about 4" (10 cm) of mulch and you'll kill the weeds, too, and drastically reduce your need to water.

**41**

*The garden cress is harvested—now we'll set out the celery.*

**Properties of different mulches.**

| MULCH MATERIAL | PROPERTIES |
| --- | --- |
| Grass cuttings | Best! Breaks down into lovely humus in record time. Also fertilizes in as quickly as a week or two if the layer of mulch is kept damp. |
| Straw | Good, even for the vegetable patch. It's preferable to leave the bales outside for a season before using them as mulch. |
| Hay | Can be used as mulching material, even though it does contain plenty of weed seeds. |
| Leaves | All types of leaves are welcome. Oak leaves, however, take a long time to break down, so it's best to shred them with a lawnmower, or mix them with other leaves and fresh grass clippings. |
| Pulled weeds | Perfect! They provide soil with plenty of nutrients, just like fresh grass clippings. The thinner the weeds are shredded, the quicker the soil can use their nutrients. All weeds can be used for mulching. |
| Wood chips and bark | I do not recommend these! Bark and wood chips drain nitrogen from the soil as they break down, so a nutrient deficiency will be evident in the first and maybe the second year. It's better to cover walking paths with this material. It can be shoveled up to cover the beds once it has broken down completely. |
| Seaweed | Blessed by the gods! Seaweeds are rich in nutrients and loosen the soil, making it fantastic to work with. Unfortunately, it has occasionally been shown to contain cadmium (a contaminant), especially in the south of Sweden. |

## SLUG PROBLEMS

But my friends, we have a problem—a real problem—the Spanish slug, nicknamed the "killer slug" by Swedes. Unfortunately, slugs and mulching aren't always a good combination. You lose sight of the slugs when they're covered by mulch, making it more challenging to fight them.

You can still amend the soil with grass clippings if you have an issue with slugs. Here's how to do it: Scatter fresh grass clippings over the area, about ⅓" to ¾" thick. Use a cultivator or a rake to mix the clippings in with the topsoil; that way there's no layer for the slugs to hide under. Meanwhile the clippings feed the soil. Scatter some new clippings as soon as the old ones have broken down.

Slugs go into hiding whenever summers are dry. That's the time to mulch as much as you can, preferably with fresh grass clippings. (Read more about grass clippings on p. 52). Slugs are dormant in the winter, so you can resume normal mulching.

Funnily enough, mulching with partially decomposed matter can also work as a slug trap, but only if you check religiously every morning and night to get rid of them. If you don't, you'll end up with a slug breeding operation.

It is indeed possible to control these pests—my community garden association has managed, through committed hunting, to slash the slug numbers down to almost nothing. That's why I have started, ever so slowly, to mulch again.

### HOW TO FIGHT SLUGS

• Hunt the slugs at dawn and at dusk; bring along a flashlight and a pair of scissors. Cut the slugs in half and leave them there. The next morning, they'll be gone or will have dried up.

- Set beer traps. Collect some shallow plastic containers with lids. Cut out entry holes on all four sides of the container. Bury the containers half way down into the soil such that the holes are at ground level and fill them with beer. Empty the containers every day, or every other day, and fill them with fresh beer.

- Paths covered with wood chips or bark keep slugs away, as do raised beds edged with planks.

- Tar paper on top of edging planks works well. Nail or staple it down and let it trail over the sides by about 2" to 2 ¾" (5 cm to 7 cm). It will take a lot for a slug to crawl across this rough paper.

- Slug bait containing iron phosphate will get rid of about 70 percent of slugs, and it is sanctioned in organic gardening. Sprinkle a tiny amount of it each time, preferably under leaves or other ground cover so that the bait doesn't get washed away. I usually put a few grains under some black plastic pots that I tip on their sides. That way the ground cover is secured.

- Nematodes, introduced when watering, will go after young slugs first and foremost. While this method works, it's tricky to get it right.

## COMPOSTING

Many of you gardeners will know this stuff inside and out. But maybe a few of you haven't gotten started yet, so let's begin from the very top.

There are two main types of compost: *Garden compost* and *kitchen compost*. Garden compost is open and dedicated to garden waste; kitchen compost is closed and is only for kitchen waste.

Create balance in the compost pile.

| NITROGEN-RICH WASTE (GREEN) | CARBON-RICH WASTE (YELLOW) |
|---|---|
| Fresh grass clippings | Dry leaves |
| Stable-animal manure | Straw |
| Vegetable/animal food scraps | Peat |
| Green herbs | Newspaper |
| Green weeds | Bark |
| Seaweed | Wood chips |
| Windfall | Dry grass |

The following is what is required for the breakdown of waste material to occur:

**Oxygen:** Worms and microorganisms require oxygen to do their job. Without them, there will be no decomposing.

**Humidity:** The material must be damp, but not soaked. It should feel like a wrung-out sponge.

**Heat:** A compost pile needs to be at least 50°F (10°C) for microorganisms to do their work. When decomposition has begun, the temperature will rise. Breakdown happens quickest when the temperature is around 122°F (50°C).

**Chemical balance:** Nitrogen-rich (green) and the carbon-rich (yellow) waste must be in balance.

### GARDEN COMPOST

For a 5,382 square foot (500 square meter) garden, you'll need a container with a capacity of 132 gallons (500 liters). Preferably it should have two compartments, one of which is dedicated to holding the compost while it matures. Better yet, you can have two compost bins. You can build your own containers cheaply by setting three pallet rims on top of each other. Collapsible mesh composters are also easy on the wallet.

*You can grow crops in mesh composters once they're full. But you'll need 6" (15 cm) of soil first.*

Situate your garden compost in a shady area, and at a proper distance from the nearest tree—outside its canopy's drip line. Do not put kitchen waste in the garden compost, because it will attract rodents. Also, doing so is prohibited [in Sweden].

Many people complain that nothing seems to happen in the compost bin. That is because, oftentimes, the mix is incorrect. Think in colors! Garden compost should contain green, yellow, and a small amount of brown. Fresh herbs are green. Straw and other dry matter are yellow. Earth, stable-animal manure, and old compost are brown. The most common culprit of slow decomposition is adding in too much of the yellow matter.

## CONTAMINATION AND WEEDS

Most disease organisms die at temperatures over 131°F (55°C). This means that most of the bad guys, in fact, die in the compost—if it's well tended, that is. But there are viruses, fungal spores, and disease-causing bacteria that do survive elevated temperatures. First and foremost, these include club root, potato late blight, potato wart disease (also known as black scab), cottony rot (also known as white mold), and tobacco mosaic virus. If you know that any of these diseases are present, throw all the pulled plants and vegetable matter in the garbage.

However, all weeds can be composted, even creeping bellflower, couch grass, ground elder—also called bishop's weed—and other challenging plants. If you're worried that they'll take root, just leave them in the sun to wilt and dry up before you add them. Another method is to set up an "in between" collection station, such as a box or a barrel, where the weeds can stay for a few days and wilt, i.e., die, before you throw them onto the compost pile.

**What belongs in garden compost:**
- Grass clippings and leaves
- Harvest waste, pulled weeds, and clumps of grass
- Finely chopped branches
- Animal manure
- Seaweed
- Straw, bark, wood chips, hay
- Dirt from flower pots
- Cat litter

### HOW TO COMPOST GARDEN WASTE

**Cover the bottom** of the compost bin with branches and twigs. If you're using a mesh composter, line it with black garden fabric or plastic to prevent it from drying out too quickly.

**Layer** garden waste (yellow and green) with thin layers of soil, stable-animal manure, or humus from last year's compost (brown). The different layers of garden waste should be about 2" to 4" (5 cm–10 cm) thick. The layers of dirt and manure need only be about ⅓"–⅔" thick. Push a garden fork down into it and shake it up a bit.

**Worms** usually turn up of their own accord. If not, you can add *Eisenida foetida*, the dung worm.

*Why don't we use dung worms more often? They're masters at composting waste.*

This is an earthworm you'll find in piles of manure or in your neighbor's compost pile. You'll recognize the dung worm by its reddish brown and skinny appearance. You can even send for them (they're sold online). Other worms are also good, but the dung worm is best at breaking down garden waste.

**Cover the compost pile** with some carpeting or plastic sheeting over the winter months. This will prevent the nutrients from being washed away when it rains.

**Dig** the compost in spring. If you have two containers or compartments, transfer the compost into the empty bin, and leave it there to mature so it breaks down completely.

### KITCHEN COMPOST

You'll need a closed container for your kitchen compost, and if you're using it year-round it must also be insulated. Check with your local council to find out what rules and regulations apply, and which type of container is permitted.

This process always works better in a big container, so choose a bin that can hold 80 gallons (300 liters) or more, even if you're only a two- or three-person household. Make sure that the container is mouse and rat proof. The container should have two compartments, preferably, one of which is dedicated to ageing compost. You can also use two containers instead of two compartments.

Because kitchen waste is rich in nitrogen, it must be balanced with carbon-rich matter such as litter or pellets. These types of material absorb excess liquid and aerate the waste, which is both wet and squishy. Garden centers sell bags of composting litter; you can also use sawdust, dry leaves, straw (which must be chopped first), wood chips, or in a pinch, shredded newspaper and egg cartons. Dirt and peat won't work because they weigh down the waste.

What belongs in the kitchen compost:
- All animal and vegetable food waste
- Paper towels and paper tissues
- Cut flowers
- Litter from pet cages and floor litter from hen houses
- Shredded egg cartons

## HOW TO COMPOST KITCHEN WASTE

1. **Cover the bottom of the container** with twigs and cut branches. It's good to add a bucketful of old compost.
2. **Chop the waste finely.** Decomposition will happen more quickly if you do. Cut carrots, potatoes, apples, and bread rolls into two to four pieces.
3. **Add composting litter** each time you empty the compost bucket. Three parts waste matter to one part litter is just about right. Stir. Cover the surface, too, with a bit of litter.
4. **Add worms.** Dung worms work well in all composting situations except for in compost tumblers. The worms lie at the bottom, sweating, when the temperature is too elevated. They set to work immediately when the temperature drops. When you empty one container into another, transfer some of the worms to the new container. If you want the worms to multiply quickly, do not disturb them unnecessarily by digging deeply too often.
5. **Air the compost pile** about once a week by stirring it with a stick or a compost aerator. This increases the flow of oxygen and prevents bad odors from developing.
6. **Fill the compost bin** to the brim. If you have two containers or two compartments, continue by filling the second one and leaving the compost in the first bin to mature until it has broken down completely. You can let the compost age in an open garden compost pile, or, if you only have one container or compartment, in a sack or barrel.
7. **If the temperature of the waste matter won't rise,** it's probably either too dry or too wet. If it's too wet, add in some compost litter. If it's dry, add in water and stir. It's also either too wet or not stirred properly if it smells bad. Add in more litter and stir energetically. The smell of ammonia usually indicates that there is too much nitrogen-rich waste. The same applies here—more stirring with added compost litter will do the trick.
8. Flies and mosquitoes will sometimes lay their eggs in the compost. Just stir with litter and then cover with litter. If you notice ants, it's because the compost is dry; add water and stir. Many complain about mold in the compost, but mold is normal.

## USE THE COMPOST'S SOIL

Soil from the garden compost is nutrient-poor, but it contributes a lot of humus components. However, soil from the kitchen compost contains lots of nutrients.

The compost soil can be spread out both while ripe (crumbly and completely decomposed), or unripe (just half-broken down). Ripe compost soil is spread in the spring, preferably, and is raked into the top soil. Unripe compost soil is best spread in the fall; that way it has time to reach an acceptable state of maturity prior to the next growing season. Another option is to mulch between the rows with the half-decomposed material.

If you're gardening with cheap, bagged soil made mostly with peat, compost soil will work wonders. If possible, add in a fourth of composted matter. For plants and houseplants, a quarter part of compost is also plenty. However, it must be fully decomposed and sieved.

## *BOKASHI*—INDOOR COMPOSTING

There is only one way to compost indoors that doesn't create problems such as flies or offen-

*A rooftop garden in Bangkok, where the household waste is composted and used to fertilize the beds.*

*Bokashi is the best method for composting indoors: no flies and no odors.*

sive smells. It's Japanese in origin and is called *bokashi*. The method involves fermenting waste in an airtight bucket. The waste is layered with bran litter made from microorganism called EM (Effective Microorganisms).

The smell of the waste disappears after a few weeks. The only odor left is from fermentation, at which point it's time to bury the waste in the garden beds or in the greenhouse.* There, decomposition continues and the matter quickly turns to humus. Many empty the fermented waste into a sack and save it for the warmer weather if the ground is still frozen.

Remember that the waste does not break down in the bucket. However, fermentation hastens the process. Fermentation also means that the waste is not quite as attractive to vermin.

---

*I've read cautions that this waste is still so acidic that plant roots should not come in contact with it for two to four weeks.

*Bokashi* buckets feature a tap, which allows you to draw liquid from it to use as food for your plants. However, this fermenting liquid must be diluted with water at a ratio of 100:1. The liquid is not odorless, but it is an excellent watered-in fertilizer.

## FERTILIZING

How much should you fertilize? It's a bit annoying that I can't provide an exact answer, as I always get asked this question whenever I give talks. Fertilizer requirements depend on so many factors: temperature, light, growth, precipitation … and when we're talking about using stable-animal manure, it's important to know what was used as litter.

So how do you do it? To begin, you'll have to be satisfied with my general advice, and/or check what's on the bag if you're using commercially bagged fertilizer. As time goes on, I hope you'll

**Learn to read the plants.**

| SIGN | REASON | ACTION |
|---|---|---|
| The plants are too green and extremely lush | Too much fertilizer | Stop all fertilizing; even mulching with grass clippings |
| The plants are puny and pale. Lettuce and spinach bolts early. Radishes are tiny and very hot. | The plants are suffering from malnutrition. It might be due to drought, cold, or compacted soil. It can also be due to insufficient fertilizing. | Have the plants been exposed to drought or cold? Is the soil compacted? If the answer is "no," then you have not fertilized enough. FERTILIZE! |

take an interest in learning how to read the health of a plant by checking the state of its leaves (see the information sidebar on above). It isn't difficult, but may be ta bit unfamiliar at first.

Insufficient feeding doesn't just make for puny growth. The small resulting yield that's in your basket will taste nasty, too. For instance, a radish that's had too little fertilizer will have small, woody roots and its flavor will be peppery and spicy. However, applying too much fertilizer can be just as bad. Potatoes that have seen too much nitrogen will have a bitter aftertaste. And don't get me started on over-fertilized spinach....

The level of nitrates increases in beets, chard, lettuce, and spinach if you over fertilize them. Nitrates can turn into nitrites, which are toxic and carcinogenic. Excessive fertilizing is also an environmental problem, because it can leak into the water supply. Last but not least, too little and too many nutrients increase the risk of disease and attacks.

### REGULAR FERTILIZING GUIDELINES

In hobby gardening, there are two main thoughts regarding fertilizing protocol. The first assumes that you have access to animal manure. The second assumes you have access to fresh grass clippings.

These two protocols can be combined. If you don't have enough grass clippings at your disposal, add in some manure; and if you lack enough manure, add in some fresh grass clippings. You can even enhance it with "gold water" (urine) or with some of the organic products available in stores. Regardless of which method you use, here are the rules to follow:

**Fertilize according to the size of your harvest.** The more you harvest, the more you should fertilize. Large vegetables and plants that grow over an extended period of time require more nutrients than a measly row of radishes. If you plant a second time, you'll need to fertilize a second time. When I sow again after an early summer's spinach harvest, I add in more fertilizer. I do it again when I add new plants.

**Distinguish between all-purpose fertilizer and short-term boosting.** Soil building and all-purpose fertilizing is done in spring and adds all-round nutrition. Short-term boosting is applied during the summer to nutrient-hungry plants. Short-term fertilizer needs to be fast acting and nitrogen-rich.

**Apply small amounts, but apply often.** Plants require frequent feedings, just like you and me. That's why it's always better to fertilize them often, but only apply a little at a time. This doesn't mean you should run yourself ragged feeding your plants day in and day out. But it is a good idea to apply both a soil-building fertilizer in the spring, and then to water in short-term boosts a few times during the height of summer.

**Learn to read the plant.** A plant that is given too little nourishment will stop growing. It will also lack flavor. Learn to read the signs that indicate a lack or excess of nutrients. Check the table at the top of the p. 50.

## ALL-PURPOSE FERTILIZING

Take care of all-purpose fertilizing in the spring. This will give your plants a blowout meal that will keep on providing nice, balanced nutrition during the larger part of the summer. Stable-animal manure is perfect for this purpose. This is an all-round fertilizer that also contains lots of humus components. Composted animal manure, which is sold commercially in bags, will do. But it includes a great deal of peat and so is not quite as nutrient-rich. You can spread extra animal manure if you sow or plant out new plants.

Stable-animal manure comes from horses, cows, pigs, sheep, or fowl. Nutrient content varies depending on what type of litter (wood shavings, peat moss, etc.) it contains. Stable-animal manure containing wood shavings should be composted for a year before it is used as fertilizer. If not, you run the risk for a temporary lack of nutrients in the bed.

Fowl manure is different from other types of manure because it contains a bit more nitrogen and works extremely quickly, but it provides hardly any humus components.

The best is ripening or composted cow or horse manure. Ripening means that it has gone through the first phase of decomposition. Composted manure is completely decomposed and crumbly like earth.

You can fertilize with fresh stable-animal manure, but it might be sticky and difficult to spread evenly. If you do, spread it early in the spring so it is easier to handle. Or preferably, compost it over a season.

Spread stable-animal manure early in spring. When spreading it in the fall, half of the nutrients will often wash away with the rain. You can only spread manure in the fall successfully if you're up north where the ground frost penetrates the earth.

When putting down all-purpose fertilizer, use a maximum of 6 ½ lbs. (3 kg) per 10 ¾ sq. ft. (1 sq. meter). You'll never use more than 6 ¾ fl. oz. (2 dl) per 10 ¾ sq. ft. (1 sq. meter) when using fowl manure. Follow the instructions on the packaging if you buy bagged fowl manure. All manure is mixed with the soil, i.e., mixed into the topsoil.

If you're sowing or planting a new batch, you can mix in 2 ¼–4 ½ lb. (1–2 kg) more stable-animal manure, or 3 ¼ fl. oz. (1 dl) of fowl manure.

## TOP DRESSING

Nitrogen-hungry crops need a quick boost of nitrogen during the summer. You can do this by applying a top dressing. This means that you water the plants with a quick-acting liquid fertilizer. Do this approximately every other week—with exception of late fall—as long as something grows in the bed. You'll make the fertilizing water yourself—a recipe for it follows below.

**Liquid poultry top dressing.** Place a few handfuls of poultry manure in a bucket of water and stir. After 24 hours, dilute the liquid with water until it is the color of strong tea. It's ready to use!

**Nettle water.** Fill a barrel with water and as many fresh nettles as the barrel will hold. Stir occasionally. Strain the nettles out after a few days. Dilute the liquid until it looks like strong tea. This produces a mild nutrient solution. A comfrey solution—a tomato favorite!—can be made the same way!

**Gold water.** Mix 1 part urine with 9 parts water and use it for watering. Don't water on top of edible crops, but in between the rows, and lightly work it into the soil. Gold water is our purest fertilizer, as long as the donor is healthy.

## GRASS CLIPPINGS

All fertilizer worries are solved if you have access to fresh grass clippings. These clippings are top-notch, complete and rich in nutrients, and provide lots of humus components. You don't have to worry about all-purpose fertilizing or top dressing. If the soil is kept damp you'll see results within a week—plants that have been moping will start to shoot up like weeds.

If you don't have any grass clippings but have plenty of ground elder (bishop's weed) and other green herbs, use them instead. First, chop them up with the lawnmower, and then use them the same way as grass clippings. If you don't have any clippings at all when your first plants begin to grow, start out with some stable-animal manure or gold water and add some clippings later.

## A WARNING ABOUT LIMING

It's madness to routinely apply lime to soil. It will cause total imbalance if you add calcium to soil when it doesn't need it. I have made that mistake, and I will never do it again. Nothing grew. This was twenty-five years ago, and I have never limed a soil since.

In reality, soils that are cultivated organically and that are rich in humus hardly ever need to be limed. In these cases the pH (the scale that indicates how acidic or alkaline the soil is) takes care of itself.

So forget what's written about gardening with regard to this and that vegetable requiring a certain pH value. All that knowledge is based on gardening that depends on artificial fertilizer.

If your soil is rich and the plants are healthy and thriving, you really don't need to fret over pH values. You don't even have to check it. Instead, continue to add organic matter each year.

*The water for top dressing is ready once it begins to stink. The nettles and ground elder (bishop's weed) are strained out.*

However, what if nothing grows even after adding stable-animal manure, compost, and humus components? Check with your neighbors and see if they know their pH value. Or test it yourself. If it's below 5–5.5 (which is extremely rare), go ahead and apply lime. Use dolomite lime or pulverized limestone. Leave a month between liming and fertilizing.

## GROWING SCHEDULES AND CROP ROTATION METHODS

In the past, I often avoided mentioning crop rotation during my lectures, and I wasn't exactly gung-ho when it came to practicing those principles myself. But this was before my crop was hit with bean yellow mosaic virus (BYMV), which

| FERTILIZER | DESCRIPTION | APPLICATION |
|---|---|---|
| Algae product [Algomin, in Sweden] | Made from algae, it contains mostly lime but also phosphorus, some nitrogen and minerals. | This is primarily a liming product. It can be used as an all-purpose fertilizer, but only if you're sure the soil is acidic. |
| Ash | Contains plenty of calcium, potassium, but also some phosphorus. Do not use ash from treated wood, as it contains toxic substances. | At most, work in 2 1/4 lb. (1 kg) per 10 3/4 sq. ft. (1 sq. meter) of soil. Also very good for berry bushes and tomatoes. |
| Bone meal | Very rich in phosphorus but also nitrogen, and some potassium. It lasts a few years. | Can be used for all-purpose fertilizing. Especially good for fruiting flowering plants. Best for potted plants. |
| Biokol [Swedish] charcoal | This is identical to charcoal. It is not a fertilizer, but it does increase the soil's fertility, due to charcoal's sponge-like ability to retain both water and nutrients. It is an economical nutrition that decreases the leaching of nutrients while at the same time much improving the structure of the soil. | Must be crushed and mixed with manure, preferably gold water. Spread 2 1/4 lb. to 11 lbs. (1–5 kg) per 10 3/4 sq. ft. (1 sq. meter) and mix in with the topsoil. |
| Grass clippings | A complete fertilizer. Fast acting, but needs humidity to decompose and provide nutrition. | Place a 2" (5 cm) layer of clippings between the rows. Add the same amount again once this layer has decayed. No other fertilizer is required. Potatoes and legumes only need this done once. |
| Green manure, cover crops | You sow plants, which are then mixed into the soil. The plant matter fertilizes the soil and their roots loosen the soil. | Everything about usage and sowing can be found on p. 96. |
| Horse manure | Total nutrition. Somewhat quicker acting and richer in nitrogen than cow manure. | Composted or ripened horse manure is excellent for all-purpose fertilizing. Spread 6 1/2 lb. (3 kg) per 10 3/4 sq. ft. (1 sq. meter). |
| Poultry manure | Much more concentrated than cow or horse manure. Extremely rich in nitrogen. | Can be used in all-purpose fertilizing, but is best for top dressing. Good for potted plants. Use a maximum of 3/4 cup per 10 3/4 sq. ft. (1 sq. meter). |
| Cow manure | Complete fertilizer. | See horse manure! |
| Compost soil from kitchen compost | The content can vary, but it's much richer in nutrients than soil from garden compost. | Can be used for all-purpose fertilizing. Spread freely, but by all means complement it with some stable-animal manure. |
| Stone meal | Contains potassium, calcium silicon, and many other trace minerals, which are often lacking in soil. It lasts for several years. | Better soil amendment than regular fertilizer. Use at any time. Extremely beneficial. Finely milled is best. Drill companies carry stone meal. |
| Urine | Total, quick-acting, and extremely rich in nutrients, especially nitrogen. | Is used primarily for top dressing, and never directly on edible plant matter. Dosage—see p. 51. |

*These healthy, good-looking root vegetables are the result of, among other things, a four-year crop rotation plan.*

turns the bean plant yellow in July. No beans for me that year, that was for sure. This yellow mosaic virus overwinters in the soil. If you grow the same plants in the same space the following year, the problems will be exacerbated.

That's the main reason—the risk of disease— why we should rotate our planting sites. Another is that certain nutrients may become depleted.

No, crop rotation makes things more pleasant for all: plants, soil, and grower.

When we talk about crop rotation, we mean the plan we use that ensures that the same plants

*A rare view: a residential garden full of vegetables that are harvested in successive batches.*

don't get set down in the same spot in subsequent years. Professional gardeners use a six-year crop rotation. Most hobbyists practice what the growers did back in the nineteenth century, which is to follow a four-year plan. When following that plan, there should be a four-year gap before a vegetable can return to a particular growing site. My beans have to wait four years before they can set foot in the same bed again.

But it is never wrong to use a six-year crop rotation. That way you can set aside one spot for green manure, such as blue phacelia, crimson clover, or Persian clover, which all loosen and enrich the soil. You can even grow green fertilizer catch crops on a four-year schedule, but I, personally, am too stingy to do that. I'd rather grow vegetables.

If your garden space is very limited, switching growing spaces won't help because virus and fungi spores will travel between the different plots. If this is the case, it's more sensible to abstain from growing a certain type of plant altogether each year. One year you'll skip cabbage plants, the next it will be potatoes or maybe onions. If you grow in a pallet rim or other shielded bed, you won't have contamination between beds. And if the soil does become diseased, you can change it out. It's certainly a great advantage!

Be extra vigilant to stick to the four-year rule for beans, onions, potatoes, and cabbage plants (all those that belong to the same family), as there are some serious diseases that can flare up in that lot. I've already mentioned bean yellow mosaic virus. However, potato wart disease (black scab), cabbage club root, onion white rot, and potato late blight are even worse. These diseases are typically caused by plants being sowed in the same area over several years.

This is all beginning to sound quite strict. However, there is a little bit of wiggle room, which is a blessing for us year-round gardeners who have more plants and sowings to take into account when we plan our gardens.

To conclude: Vary the plantings as much as possible and try to follow a four-year rotation plan. There is room for compromise, which is shown in the information table at the bottom of this page.

### PLAN FOR A FOUR-YEAR CROP ROTATION

**Separate the plants** into four groups, preferably determined by their nutrient requirement: 1. Major requirement: squash, cabbage, celery, leeks, and cucumbers. 2. Reasonable requirement: onion, root vegetables, lettuce, dill and parsley. 3. Minimal requirement: potatoes. 4. Enriches the soil with nitrogen: beans and peas.

**Separate the beds** into four sections, one for each group. Let the groups switch places each year as shown in the columns below. Four growing beds or four pallet rims is a good solution. Make one bed for each change.

**Fertilize** group 1 the most, groups 2 and 3 a little less, group 4 the least. The beans and peas (legumes) are included in group 4. They take in nitrogen from the air, which makes them partly self-sufficient in terms of nitrogen.

Example of a four-year crop rotation.

| YEAR | 1ST CHANGE | 2ND CHANGE | 3RD CHANGE | 4TH CHANGE |
|------|-----------|-----------|-----------|-----------|
| 1 | Winter crop: cabbage plants, leeks, celery, etc. | Root vegetables, onions, squash | Early potatoes, followed by catch or cover crop | Peas and beans |
| 2 | Root vegetables, onion, squash | Early potatoes, followed by catch or cover crop | Peas and beans | Winter crop: cabbage plants, leeks, celery, etc. |
| 3 | Early potatoes followed by catch or cover crop | Peas and beans | Winter crop: cabbage plants, leeks, celery, etc. | Root vegetables, onions, squash |
| 4 | Peas and beans | Winter crop: cabbage plants, leeks, celery, etc. | Root vegetables, onions, squash | Early potatoes, followed by catch or cover crop |

Grow winter vegetables collectively in one bed. I'm thinking of kale, Brussels sprouts, celeriac, black kale, and leeks, which hopefully will yield a harvest sometime in the winter. They all gorge on nutrients so it's advantageous to keep them in the same bed. That way I can give them a little bit of extra care when it gets chilly, cover them against the cold, and maybe protect them against deer.

Spinach, chard, and lettuce are free agents and can grow anywhere. You can even allow other quick crops, such as garden cress, arugula, and dill to grow in the wrong space, but not year after year in the same spot.

Adjust the plan to suit your needs. Maybe you don't want to grow potatoes and would prefer to grow green manure instead. That's absolutely no problem! If your squash plants can't fit into one growing shift, let them have two.

Perennial vegetables always have their own bed where they grow year after year, often alongside perennial flowers or herbs. Consequently, they don't belong in the system I describe here.

### SHORTCUTS TO SUPER SOIL

By now you might believe that it's really complicated to create fertile soil. That's not true at all. If you wish, you can use a shortcut. Here you go:

1. **Dig** one spade depth in late fall. If the soil is light, dig it in the spring. If the soil is porous, you can get away with just loosening it up in the spring.

2. **Winter mulch** with leaves, hay, straw, seaweed, semi-decayed compost, pulled weeds, or other plant matter. This will stop the nutrients from leaching out, something that can happen if the winter is wet.

3. **Rake off the remains of the mulch** and fertilize with animal manure (see p. 50) a few weeks before planting time. In springtime, the earth is airy and crawling with worms. While you're at it, mix in as much compost as you wish.

4. **Mulch** during growing season (if you don't have a big slug problem). Grass clippings are especially good, as they are quickly broken down to humus and enrich the soil. But don't mulch until growth starts in the bed in spring/early summer. Place the mulch in between the rows, and keep an eye on the birds so they don't make a mess of the mulch and snuff out delicate plants. Also, keep an eagle eye out for slugs!

5. **Treat** the soil with organic waste. Once the soil is dark and has a crumbly texture, you don't have to feed it as much humus. But for heaven's sake, don't stop feeding the soil humus components or it will go back to its former, inferior quality.

*Right: Borlotti beans and all other beans are grown in the same growing period as peas, i.e., legumes.*

# SPRING GARDENING

**SPRING IS TEMPERAMENTAL; IT'S ALL WARMTH AND EUPHORIA ONE DAY, AND ICY, NORTHERLY WINDS THE NEXT. BUT NOTHING WILL HOLD US BACK!**

ACCORDING TO METEOROLOGICAL data, spring begins in Stockholm in the middle of March. But we wouldn't dream of planting outside. The soil is icy cold and wet. There are blasts of sun, of course, but you can bet there will be snow the following week, so it's better to wait before sowing.

That same statistical chart says that spring comes to Luleå [northern Sweden], my childhood hometown, on April 20. But even the residents of Luleå have to wait a good month before the kick-off of the growing season. Say WHAT? Do we really have a whole month without harvesting, without gardening? Not necessarily. I see these options:

**Indoor gardening** is productive, even in spring. Why not start another set of microgreens? (p. 136).

**A "heated" cold frame—also called a hotbed or a hot box**—grants access to greenery, provided you've prepared the frame during late winter. But it isn't too late to build one now (see p. 126). It will be very useful to you well into summer, especially in the north of Sweden.

**Parsnip and Jerusalem artichokes,** which have overwintered in the ground, are extremely tasty at this time of year. But they must be harvested in early spring, otherwise they might bolt (start flowering) and their roots will become tough wooden logs.

**Perennial vegetables** will be ready to show up any day now. I usually throw down a row cover to hurry things along.

Overwintered kale plants are burgeoning—they're sending up delicate pale green shoots. This is a delicacy you won't find even in the fanciest of eating establishments. In the south of Sweden you can also enjoy young, delicate chard and Belgian endives, and overwintered mâche.

## INDOOR SEED STARTING

However, the harvest is not our highest priority at the moment. Right now it's seed starting, or, as it's called in the trade, pre-cultivation. It's a way of getting ahead by starting to grow indoors in order to produce an earlier harvest. Pre-cultivation is sometimes necessary to ensure that plants have time to fully develop in our [Nordic] climate. Take chili peppers: We wouldn't get a

*Left: Lettuce is not planted in the ground until night temperatures have reached 41°F (5°C) or higher.*

solitary fruit without pre-cultivation. Chilies are special also in that you can start sowing them almost as early as you like, as long as you use grow lights.

On the cheat sheet on p. 14, you'll see if a plant needs to be pre-cultivated, or if it can be sown directly outdoors. This information will also be on the seed packet. There are basically four plant categories that typically are pre-cultivated:

**Plants that require a long time to develop.** These plants won't be ready for picking if you don't get a leg up by starting them early. Examples are eggplant, celery and celeriac, chili peppers and bell peppers, artichokes, leeks and other seed-sown onions, and tomatoes. All require pre-cultivation.

**Cucumbers, squashes, and pumpkins.** These plants grow fast, but their seeds rot in cold soil and their tender leaves hate the cold. You can only sow these plants directly outdoors in the south of Sweden.

**Lettuces and other fast-growing plants can also be pre-cultivated.** We do this so we can harvest them a few weeks early. I personally insist on pre-cultivating parsley and loose-leaf lettuces. But heads up! Cold weather plants that have a short life span, such as arugula, sandwich cress, cilantro, and dill should never be pre-cultivated,

because you'll hardly have time to get them into the ground before they bolt! They're often sold commercially as plants—that's a waste!

As you know, we don't sow **potatoes.** But setting aside potatoes for sprouting is still pre-cultivating. It's best if the sprouts are in the light. Preferably, put them in an egg carton with some soil, or on a tray with some soil. That way the potatoes will grow sprouts as well as roots.

### TIME TO PRE-CULTIVATE—BUT WHEN?

There are lunatics—of which I am one—who start pre-cultivating on Christmas Day. But to be more practical, as well as to be more confident in the end-result, you should wait until spring. Of course it's great to have huge plants, but it's not fun when you start getting pushed out of your home. Besides, pre-cultivated plants have more trouble acclimatizing to the outdoors. This is especially true for cucumber and squash plants.

A plant's maturation period (refer to the cheat sheet on p. 14) will tell you when it's time to start sowing. If the plant requires only two months to grow, like the cucumber, I won't start it until the beginning of May. That will give the plant time to produce many cucumbers. However, a chili pepper takes twice the time to develop, so I'll plant it two months earlier, if not even earlier.

| When to start pre-cultivation. | | |
|---|---|---|
| **PLANT GROUP** | **SOUTHERN SWEDEN** | **NORTHERN SWEDEN** |
| Chili pepper, bell pepper, eggplant, artichoke, celery | Jan–March | Feb–March |
| Leek | Feb | March |
| Tomato plants | Feb–March | March–April |
| Scallion, Chinese chive, and other seed-sown onions | March | April |
| Basil, cucumber, fennel, cabbage, parsley, pumpkin, sweet corn, squash | April | May |
| Lettuce, chard, and other quick-growing, cold weather plants, potatoes (sprouting) | April | May |

*Even potatoes are pre-cultivated, preferably on top of about one inch of soil in an egg carton or on a tray.*

A basic rule: Sow too late rather than too early. I hardly ever hear griping from gardeners who have started too late, but there is a steady litany of complaints from those who began too early.

By all means, consult the table on the left. It will show you approximately when you can start pre-cultivating different types of kitchen plants.

### THE MAIN PRINCIPLES OF PRE-CULTIVATING
Beginners often grumble that their plants are undersized. Naturally they don't have to be as plump as the specimens from the nursery, but they should be upright and be able to support themselves. One typical reason they're spindly is weak light exposure, and/or an overly heated room. Let the three principles of pre-cultivating be your guide, and things will work out fine.

**Lots of light** is the first principle. There won't be a whole lot of photosynthesis taking place if there isn't enough light, and that can subsequently lead to weak plants. But luckily, plants happen to thrive even in artificial light, i.e., under grow lights. This makes it possible to successfully grow plants by a window as well as in a dark basement. You can read more about grow lights on p. 67.

**Correct temperature** is the second principle. While seeds germinate well at room temperature, plants prefer a few degrees less. If the room is too warm, it's important to have extra light, due to this interesting relationship: The higher the indoor temperature, the higher the need for light. Inversely, the worse the lighting conditions, the lower the temperature needs to be. That means we can balance temperature with appropriate lighting to allow spindly plants grow sturdy.

**Keeping the humidity level** steady is the third principle. Small seeds do not tolerate the slightest drought. But just as quickly as they can dry up and die, they can rot and die, so water them just enough, and only if the soil begins to dry out.

### FORCING PLANTS—A STEP-BY-STEP
**1. Sow in pots**—they need not to be taller than 2" (5 cm). Milk cartons work well; cut them down to size and snip off the corners at the bottom, too. Cell pack inserts are excellent for those who cultivate a lot, because you end up with lots of plants, and their roots are not disturbed when planted out. Cell packs are especially well suited to cabbage and root vegetable plants.

**2. Fill up with potting mix** or sifted cactus soil that is low in nutrients. If the seeds are small and expensive, you can add a little perlite or vermiculite to the potting mix. Both are volcanic products that will aerate the soil. You can even sow in seed starter mix or potting soil, especially if the seeds are big, but remove the clumps of peat beforehand. A smart solution is to fill the bottom half the pot with seed starting soil that contains nutrients, and top it with potting soil. That way the plant will have access to nutrients once it grows big enough to need it.

*There are no better pots for tomato seedlings than milk cartons.*

3. **Spread out the seeds** thinly and cover them with soil—to a depth of four to five times the size of the seed. Tap the pot against the side of the table; this will make the soil settle just right. Water carefully so you don't wash away the seeds. You can also water by showering the sown seeds. Mark the pots with the plant's name.

4. **Place the pots** in a mini greenhouse. Air them by placing a wedge between the lid and the box, or the seeds will grow moldy. The seeds grow well at room temperature, but they'll do even better if you place them in a furnace room or elsewhere that's warm. You can also place your plantings on an electric heating mat or in a bottom-heated mini greenhouse.

*Buy cell pack inserts—it's a smart way to start plants. You'll get lots!*

5. **Once the seeds** have germinated, place them in a window that gets lots of light. If you don't have a sunny window, you'll need a strip light. But even a south-facing window will not provide enough light if you sow in late winter, so your room's temperature will have be lowered a little. Most of us don't have such a space, so just turn off the heater that's under the window.

6. **Repot** the seedlings in their own individual pots once the first true leaves have developed. The "true" leaves are those that develop after the tiny heart-shaped ones appear—cotyledons—at the base of the stalk. Normally we give each plant its own pot, but we'll let plants that grow in tufts, such as Chinese chives, mizuna cabbage, leaf lettuce, regular chives, and basil share a common pot. Now fill the pots with seed starting or potting soil; make a hole in the soil with a pencil and place the plant/plants there and pack the soil lightly all around. Finish by watering. Light is still required and the temperature should preferably be a few degrees below room temperature. Let the soil dry out a little between waterings.

7. **Large plants** often need a second repotting into larger containers. However, this is only done if the root ball takes up the entire pot. Pull the root ball out a little to check and see if the soil is packed through with roots.

8. **Harden off** the plants before planting them outside; this allows them to gradually get used to the outdoor climate. Let them sit outside (but protected from the wind and in the shade) for just under a week. The leaves will become strong enough to tolerate sunshine, and then the plant will be ready for life outdoors.

9. Plant outside when it's overcast and the risk of frost is gone. Warm weather plants need a

*Time for repotting. Each plant gets its individual pot with planting soil.*

nighttime temperature of at least 46.4°F (8°C). Cold weather plants, like cabbage, require 41°F (5°C), but can survive lower temps. Make a hole for each plant and place it a little deeper than before (this does not apply to lettuce). Be careful so the clump of dirt doesn't fall apart. Pat the soil down around the plant with a light touch so it's steady. Water, and cover with row cover or plastic. This way the plants will take more quickly. Planting distances are shown on the "cheat sheet" on p. 14.

## GROW LIGHTS—WHICH TO CHOOSE?

Now the question is, which grow lights are the best? This is a hot topic among both growers and lighting experts. Unfortunately, there are no large-scale experiments comparing different types of lights. This might be because constant innovations are taking place at a whirlwind pace—this is especially true with LED technology. Once this book is in print, many new interesting things will probably have already happened.

On the basis of this jumble, I'm supposed to give advice; so I'll do this by bringing out everything for which there is a consensus, and for which I can vouch for through personal experience as a hobby gardener.

Let's begin by eliminating the types of lights that are of no interest to recreational gardeners. The first to go are light bulbs. They emit the wrong wavelength, their light is too weak, and they become too warm. Metal halide (halogen) and HPS (High Pressure Sodium) lights can also be discarded. They are still used in large-scale growing operations, but less and less by hobbyists. The lights are too cumbersome and gobble up lots of energy. Personally, I'm very happy to be rid of them. Just hanging them was a total nightmare, not to mention their light was very unpleasant.

Two alternatives remain: fluorescent tubular lights and LED lamps. On the plus side, both work. They're useful for forcing plants, growing microgreens indoors, and overwintering plants. They make good supplemental light for potted plants in dark rooms. All produce satisfactory light.

### PROS AND CONS OF LED

Plants like red and blue light. Photosynthesis works best at such wavelengths. The color red promotes branching, stem elongation, and root systems; while the blue light promotes sturdy plants. Most common in use are LEDs (Light Emitting Diodes) with red and blue lights, which, unfortunately, bask the room in a horrendous reddish lavender color.

We're aware now that plants also require a little bit of white light. This they will get if they are located in a window, but not if you are growing plants inside a room.

I suggest that if you go with a LED lamp, get one that also emits white light. These are now widely available on the market.

LED lamps don't give off any heat, they last a long time, and they're very energy efficient. They're easy to set up and don't require any special fixtures. The light always points down. Their drawbacks? The price. And for some, it's a problem that they're mainly sold online. Not everyone likes shopping online. Furthermore, it's difficult to find your way around the LED jungle, especially when some vendors enthusiastically promise you the moon.

## PROS AND CONS OF FLUORESCENT TUBULAR LIGHTS

Fluorescent tube lights still have a part to play, even as LED lamps are coming in strong. Tube lights work well, are relatively energy efficient, and, above all, are a lot cheaper than LED lamps. Type T5 tubes have the best light yield, but T8 works, too.

One of the disadvantages of tube lights is that you have to get a fixture kit with a reflector. Without the reflector, the light will shine in all directions and consequently you lose a lot of useful wattage. The fixture takes up space and is awkward to mount. Another drawback is that some types of fluorescent tubes contain mercury, which today we know is one the most toxic waste products in our environment. The tubes also burn out quicker than LED lamps.

## HOW ARE THE LAMPS USED?

**How many watts do you need?** Two T8 tubes at 37 watts each barely cover 10.76 sq. ft. (1 sq. meter). The same goes for two T5 tubes at 35 watts. A 30-watt LED lamp will also barely light up 10.76 sq. ft. (1 sq. meter). All lamps are suspended. It's important to check that you have a point of attachment that can handle the lamp's weight.

**How high do they hang?** Lights should hang 7 ¾" to 11 ¾" (20–30 cm) above the plants. Actually, they can hang as close to the plants as possible, as long as the lamp doesn't emit any heat. Heat will make the plants grow lanky. Move the lights further up as the plants grow taller. However, remember that plants lose light if the distance between plants and lamp increases. There isn't less total light, but the light will spread over a larger area.

**How many hours are the lamps on for?** If you're forcing plants, the lamps need to be on 14 to 16 hours per 24-hour period. It's easiest to use a timer that can be programmed to switch the lights on and off. The same applies if you grow microgreens in the winter. If you use the lights to overwinter plants, you can cut the time down to 8 to 10 hours per 24-hour period. One way to improve the light

*LED lamps have arrived and are here to stay.*

*T5 type fluorescent tube lights are also a good choice.*

is to invest in reflector material that can be placed at the back and to the sides of the plants; why not use some white cardboard lined with aluminum foil? It does make a difference.

**When do lamps get old?** If after a few years you notice that plants are not growing as nice and sturdy as before, it's probably because the lamps, especially fluorescent tubes, have lost their power. Then you might have to change the lights. Old fluorescent tubes are an environmental hazard, so they need to be handled accordingly.

**When to use less light.** Decrease lamp hours when the spring sun shines stronger and if you grow in a sunny window. I tend to turn off the lights at the beginning or middle of May.

## LET'S START SOWING OUTDOORS!

Finally! The soil is ready—it's wonderfully crumbly and its temperature is at 41°F (5°C). Most of our kitchen crops want to be sown now. I usually get off to a flying start with spinach, lettuce, radishes, peas, fava beans, dill, and arugula. A week or two later I'll sow beets and chard. Once the radishes are finished, it's usually time to sow green beans, which are a warm weather crop.

Bed sowing is a critical moment in gardening. Many gardeners fail, and then often blame the seed companies. That is seldom fair. Even if the seeds' germination rate isn't always the promised 70 to 90 percent, it's still a reasonable expectation. Oftentimes the sowing method is the culprit, i.e., it's too dry or too wet. If the seed germinates and then a drought hits, the seedling dies. It also happens that the seed or the tender seedlings drown in water and rot. So, it's well worth taking care of the little ones.

This is how you decide if it's time to bring out the seed packets and start sowing.

*We have fluorescent T8 tubes in my block's community greenhouse; they are on 14 hours per 24-hour period. We get great plants.*

**Check That the Soil Is Ready!** The soil should no longer be squishy or muddy and stick to your boots. The clumps of soil should fall apart when you work and rake the ground. In the south of Sweden, that's typically around April or May, and May or June up north.

**Check the Soil's Temperature!** If the soil is 41°F (5°C) or above and its texture is ready, it's time to sow all the cold weather plant seeds that grow in 41°F (5°C) soil. We make exceptions, however, for mizuna cabbage and other Asian leafy greens, as well as daikon

*Seeds grow best in loose, even soil. Here the soil is evened out with an Iranian garden tool.*

*Beans, just like all other seeds, are sown to a depth of four to five times the seed's diameter.*

*The rows show burgeoning growth, and I take the opportunity to lift up the row covers and thin out the seedlings.*

radish. They should be sown a week or two later, or better still, in late summer. Other seeds need warmer soil to germinate. Beans, for example, require the soil to be at least 53.6°F (12°C). You'll find germination temperatures in the cheat sheet on p. 14.

### OUTDOOR BED SOWING—STEP BY STEP

**1. Rake the soil** so it is loose and even. Don't bother to remove small stones; as long as they're not directly in the row; they are good for the soil structure. However, remove all weeds and weed roots from the soil.

**2. Time to sow.** Mark the rows with a string if you're growing in large beds. The sowing depth should be four to five times bigger than the seed's diameter. Make the row indent with a hoe, your hand, or a rake handle to the correct depth. Cover the seeds with soil. Sow thinly— it's unnecessary to throw down seeds that will only be thinned out later. Finish the sowing by pressing down the soil lightly with your hand or with the rake.

**3. Try to wide-bed sow** quick-growing vegetables such as radishes, dill, leaf lettuce, and arugula.

You don't sow in rows but scatter the seeds over a larger area. Using the back of the rake, rake up a sowing row measuring the width of the rake. Spread the seeds evenly over the surface. Rake the soil, first in one direction and then in the opposite direction, to cover the seeds.

**4. Compacted soil** is not the best for sowing. But if you fill the row with planting soil or other good soil and then sow in it, it will work better.

**5.** Finally, **water** the bed. Cover the bed with fabric row cover for a couple of weeks—that'll do the trick (see p. 29). You can mulch the ground with grass clippings or other vegetable waste once the plants have grown about 4" (10 cm) tall.

**6. Thin out** the plants once they have reached 2"-4". Their growth will be hampered if you wait too long. It feels brutal to cull half the spinach harvest. However, what you have really done is doubled the harvest. Don't throw away the thinned out plants; they're a delicacy. Thin in two batches preferably. The second time, thin out to the distance printed on the seed packet or

*Asian and African gardeners have taught us to wide-sow quick-growing leafy greens.*

in the cheat sheet on p. 14. Sometimes the weeds grow so quickly that it's difficult to tell the rows apart. This applies especially to carrots, parsnips, and parsley. Mix in some radish seeds in your sowing mix. Radishes grow quickly and help you find the row when it is time to thin out.

### INTERPLANTING YIELDS A DOUBLE HARVEST

Imagine a vegetable bed with leeks at the end of June. You'll see mostly bare soil and a few spindly leek plants. So why not follow the Chinese example and interplant a quick-growing crop between the slow-growing ones? This doubles the harvest while keeping weeds down significantly.

Here are a few examples of successful interplantings: chervil and onion sets between leeks; arugula between cabbage plants; spinach between parsnips. Once the leeks, parsnips, and cabbage start to grow and need the space, you will have already harvested the quick crop.

But don't hold back with the interplanting. Get it done as soon as possible, preferably a few weeks before the slow-growing specimens have even been planted outside.

Spinach and radishes make excellent interplantings. Little Gem, which is a miniature romaine lettuce, is also tailor-made for this purpose. I usually have forced lettuce plants, but it works perfectly well to sow them directly, too. Onion sets are just as handy. I always buy twice the amount I think I'll need, and use them for interplantings. They don't have time to get very big, but as young, tender spring vegetables, they're difficult to beat. You'll find all the plants that work as interplantings on the cheat sheet on p. 14. I have listed my own favorites at the top of the next page.

### PERENNIAL VEGETABLES

Where would the spring gardener be without perennial vegetables, i.e., those plants that return

**71**

*We must use up every inch of ground. That's why lettuce is grown in between the stalks of corn.*

| My best interplantings. |
| --- |
| Cos/romaine lettuce Little Gem |
| Dill |
| Cilantro |
| Onion (sets) |
| Turnip |
| Mizuna cabbage |
| Leaf or head lettuce |
| Arugula |
| Radish |
| Garden cress |
| Spinach |

year after year? Pretty desperate, I would think. Scallions, French sorrel, and a whole bunch of other perennial vegetables make a comeback every year. And they often do this before you've even sowed your beets and carrots. I find that comforting.

These are the easiest of all kitchen crops to grow, but it's pretty obvious that a plant that can withstand the weather of Nordic winters is easy to manage. Plant it once and you'll end up with a permanent crop. No more digging, no more thinning out, no more sowing . . . not to mention its flavor. You'll agree that there is something special about leaves that have grown in the spring sun.

Generally speaking, perennials are hardly bred and developed at all, which links them very closely to their original species. This also means that they're extra nutritious. The less breeding involved in a plant, the more nutrient-dense it is, according to nutrition experts. Perennial vegetables have a long but forgotten history. In the nineteenth century garden, thirty or so differ-

ent species were grown. They were often used as edging plants around the kitchen garden. I found out about these in texts written during that time period.

Most of these plants come up so early in the season that they almost emerge from the snow banks. My first harvest is usually at the end of April or at the beginning of May. Often I have barely begun my spring sowing when my perennial beds start to rumble. Several different types of spring onion are pushing through the soil, and the French sorrels unfold their showy leaves, not bothered in the least by the nighttime cold. Just bring out your bucket and fill it with onion greenery, with or without garlic taste, or tart, or sweet, or nutty-flavored shoots....

I'll set down my trusty bucket at the kitchen sink, where my husband starts dreaming up a delicious supper. Typically it's a whole oven-baked fish on a bed of perennial greens, where

*Right: A spring harvest of perennials: chives, French sorrel, spring onions, lungwort and stringy stonecrop.*

**72**

*In the spring, we harvest Caucasian mountain spinach, which is both a perennial and a climber.*

sorrel imparts the flavor. On other days, the fresh leaves end up in pierogi with goat cheese.

While the first perennial harvest takes place a few weeks later in the north of Sweden, it happens far earlier in the south. Harvesting continues throughout the whole summer. With a bit of additional fertilizing and TLC, it will continue into late fall.

## TART LEAVES AND BUNCHING ONIONS

In the table to the right, you'll find perennial vegetables that are worth growing and that can be harvested in the spring. I'm skipping specimens that yield ridiculously small amounts relative to the effort required to grow them. I'm thinking of skirret and earthnut peas, also called tuberous peas. Jerusalem artichokes are usually harvested in the fall, but are far tastier in the spring, so they belong in spring.

Most perennial vegetables are either leaf vegetables—greens—or bunching onions. The first to arrive among the leaves are the tart types, such as sorrel and patience dock. They have the acidity of lemons, the freshness of apples, and herby greenness of basil. They add a special dimension to everything from soups to sauces, and omelets and salads. The tartness comes from the leaves that, just like rhubarb, contain oxalic acid. That's why you don't wolf them down. In the seventeenth century, both French sorrel and patience dock where cultivated in the gardens in the Norrbotten region of Sweden. Their hardiness is therefore not something we need to worry about.

Next come the bunching onions, which are just as hardy and are grown for their green leafy stems. A few of them also produce an edible bulb. But if you eat the bulb, then you're eating the root and so you won't have any part of the plant left. By the way, all onion leaves are edible. Do a taste test, and maybe you'll discover a new gourmet onion among the 600 specimens out there. I'm convinced that different types of bunching onions are going to be the next big thing. They have all the advantages of being easy to grow, tasting great, and being awfully attractive with their tussock leaves and star-shaped flowers.

The major issue with perennials is that nurseries don't offer them for sale. Rhubarb, chives, and asparagus are out there; occasionally you can even find wood garlic, Welsh onion, and blue sea kale. So what are we to do? We place an order for them. A good company will help us find them, a not-so-great company won't.

Thank heavens we can sow most of them. Seeds can be purchased through some companies. Check online. Don't count on a harvest during the first year. The plant needs this time to develop a robust root system. But I'm sure

**Perennial salad vegetables worth growing.**

| PLANT | DESCRIPTION |
| --- | --- |
| Red-veined dock *Rumex sanguineus* | Related to sorrel, but has coarser leaves and its flavor isn't as good. However, the leaves have beautiful blood-red veins. Height: 11 ³/₄" to 15 ³/₄" (30–40 cm). Plant distance: 9 ³/₄" to 11 ³/₄" (25–30 cm). |
| Chives *Allium schoenoprasum* | Tufts with tube-shaped leaves and pink flowers. Height: 11 ³/₄" (30 cm). Plant distance: 9 ³/₄" (25 cm). Harvest in consecutive batches. |
| Jerusalem artichoke *Helianthus tuberosus* | Root vegetable with nodes that contain *inulin*, which is beneficial for diabetics. It's preferable to switch growing spaces each year or every other year and dig up all the nodes; otherwise the plant will become a nuisance weed. Harvest in late fall or spring. Plant the nodes 4" to 6" (10–15 cm) deep. Plant distance: 11 ³/₄" to 15 ³/₄" (30–40 cm). |
| Chinese chives *Allium tuberosum* | Tufts of flat, garlic-flavored leaves and white flowers. Height: 11 ³/₄" (30 cm). Sow in clumps at a distance of 9 ³/₄" (25 cm), or sow in close rows. Harvest in consecutive batches. |
| Tree onion, top setting onion *Allium x proliferum* | This onion is grown for its hollow leaves and groupings of small onions at the top. Height: 19 ¹/₂" to 27 ¹/₂" (50–70 cm). Get a seedling and plant it in spring. It's even better if you can get hold of some top onions and plant them 1 ¹/₄" (3 cm) deep, preferably a couple of them together. Remember that you can't sow tree onions. Plant distance: 11 ³/₄" (30 cm). |
| Poor man's asparagus, Good-King-Henry *Chenopodium bonus-henricus* | Belongs to the spinach family and is related to Lamb's quarter. Its large, meaty leaves can be used like spinach when new and tender. Just about impossible to kill. Height: 19 ¹/₂" to 31 ¹/₂" (50–80 cm). Plant distance: 9 ³/₄" to 11 ³/₄" (25 to 30 cm). |
| Salad burnet *Sanguisorba minor* | A medieval salad plant with a cucumber-like, nutty flavor. Height: 9 ³/₄" (25 cm). Seeds need light to germinate. This plant likes part-shade and nutrient-rich, loose soil. Plant distance: 9 ³/₄" to 11 ³/₄" (25 to 30 cm). |
| Scallion, Welsh onion *Allium fistulosum* | Clumps of hollow, gray-tinted stalks, and creamy-white flower balls. Use as salad onion. Height: 19 ¹/₂" to 31 ¹/₂" (50–80 cm). Plant distance: 11 ³/₄" (30 cm). |
| Rhubarb *Rheum rabarbarum* | This plant is grown for its stalks. Elmblitz is a variety with a low oxalic acid content. Height: 39 ¹/₂" to 78 ³/₄" (100–200 cm). You will not see any new growth if you let the rhubarb bolt. Plant distance: 39 ¹/₂" × 39 ¹/₂" (100 × 100 cm). |
| Ramsons *Allium ursinum* | Garlic-flavored wide leaves and white flowers. Height: 9 ³/₄" to 11 ³/₄" (25 to 30 cm). Likes part to full shade in humus-rich, damp soil. It's harvested in the spring and early summer. The plants will wither after flowering. Buy seedlings or sow indoors. Plant distance: 6" to 8" (15–20 cm). |
| Caucasian spinach *Hablitzia tamnoides* | A climber that can reach over 13' (4 m). In spring, the leaves are used like spinach. Afterwards, the climber should be left to develop freely. A climbing trellis will be needed. The plant requires porous soil and sunshine. You will need to sow it, as these plants are not for sale. The seeds are cold stratified by placing the pots out in the winter cold for a few weeks. When the spring sun turns warm, the seeds will germinate, typically. Plant distance: 31 ¹/₂" (80 cm). |
| Wild arugula, wild rocket *Diplotaxis tenuifolia* | Forms rosettes of leaves that taste like arugula. Height: 4" to 6" (10–15 cm). Requires sun or part-shade, and light soil. Sow indoors or direct sow. The seeds are teeny-tiny and are very thinly covered. Harvest in consecutive batches to keep the plant from bolting. Plant distance: 4" (10 cm). |
| Sand leek, rocambole *Allium scorodoprasum* | Only the ¹/₃" (1 cm) wide stalks are harvested. Even the bulbils that develop in the lilac-red flower are edible. Height: 19 ¹/₂" to 31 ¹/₂" (50–80 cm). Likes sunshine and rich soil. Reproduction takes place through onion cloves or bulbils. Sow directly once the soil is ready. Plant distance: 6" to 8" (15–20 cm). |

*cont. on the next page*

*cont. from previous page*

| PLANT | DESCRIPTION |
|---|---|
| French sorrel<br>*Rumex scutatus* | Related to wrinkled dock, the leaves are slightly citrus-flavored but less tart. It grows like a ground cover. Height: 6" (15 cm). Pre-cultivate indoors in early spring. Plant in a sunny spot, but in porous and damp soil. Harvest in consecutive batches by cutting down the plant to a 1" to 1 $^1/_2$" (a few centimeters) from the soil. |
| Garden asparagus<br>*Asparagus officinalis* | This is grown for its finger-thick shoots in spring. Develops 39$^1/_3$" to 59" (100–150 cm) high hedges that can live up to 50 years. The simplest is to buy plants, referred to as crowns with roots. They become established quickly. You'll dig a furrow for the asparagus hedge in the spring. Make it 9 $^3/_4$" (25 cm) deep and 11$^3/_4$" (30 cm) wide. Form the bottom of the furrow as a raised edge. Spread the roots in the furrow with a plant distance of 11$^3/_4$". Cover with 3$^1/_4$" (8 cm) of composted animal manure and soil. Push down the rest of the soil as the plants grow, but do not bury them! The first harvest will be in the third year. Don't let the bed get taken over by weeds. Shoots are harvested when they have reached 6" to 8" (15–20 cm). Harvest stops at midsummer. These asparagus don't need to be bleached. |
| Patience dock, garden patience<br>*Rumex patientia* | Luxurious, mildly tart leaves. These are used just like sorrel. Height: 27$^1/_2$" to 35$^1/_2$" (70–90 cm). Plant distance: 11$^3/_4$" to 15$^3/_4$" (30–40 cm). |
| Sea kale<br>*Crambe maritima* | This is primarily grown for the first spring shoots that are bleached. The silver-gray leaves are allowed to spread out—31$^1/_2$" (80 cm) in diameter—after the harvest. Height: 23$^2/_3$" to 27$^1/_2$" (60–70 cm). Bleaching: Place a bucket over the first shoots. Leave the bucket in place for 1–2 weeks. Harvest ends after a month. Plant distance: 31$^1/_2$" (80 cm). The seeds should be cold stratified. By all means sow them in pots in late winter, cover with garden fabric, and leave outside. These plants often self-seed. |
| Wrinkled dock, sorrel<br>*Rumex rugosa* | Leafy green with a tart flavor. The leaves contain oxalic acid. Height: 15$^3/_4$" to 23$^2/_3$" (40–60 cm). Plant distance: 11$^3/_4$" (30 cm). |
| Large leaf sorrel<br>*Rumex acetosa* | Wild sorrel produces a smaller harvest and is more tart tasting than the garden variety. Height: 11$^3/_4$" to 19$^1/_2$" (30–50 cm). The plant is grown like the garden sorrel. Take note that garden sorrel often is sold as large leaf sorrel. Plant distance: 9$^3/_4$" (25 cm). |

that you'll be able to wait just that little bit longer if you've been doing without sorrel up until now in your gardening life.

Perennial vegetables that would grow well are still being discovered. I personally have South Korean stringy stonecrop (*Sedum sarmentosum*) with healthy, juicy leaves in spring and early summer, followed by its sun-yellow flowers. It is my favorite groundcover. I'm trying out perennial kale at the moment. I hope it will live up to its promise.

We now have access to a true goldmine thanks to the book *Around the World in 80 Plants* by Stephen Barstow. It is a classic in the making. So let us continue to explore and experiment!

## TIPS FOR GROWING PERENNIALS

**Place** the perennial vegetables in their own bed, preferably together with perennial herbs. This is most practical way to do it since they all have more or less the same needs. Just remember that wood-stemmed plants such as thyme, lavender, and salvia require fewer nutrients than leaf-rich plants like sorrel and poor man's asparagus (Good-King-Henry). Therefore, halve the amount of fertilizer you apply to wood-stemmed plants and place them in the sunniest spot.

**A sunny site** is best, even if the green-leafy plants can tolerate part-shade.

**Airy, porous soil** is a clear advantage. The soil can be both sandy and part clay, but plants will not grow well if it's compacted.

**Fertilize in the spring** with a few shovels of animal manure per 10 ¾ sq. ft. (1 sq. meter). You can also fertilize with fresh grass clippings. You can do this by covering the soil with about 1 ¼" (a few centimeters) layer of fresh clippings. And you can can never add too much compost humus.

**Harvest in consecutive batches.** If you do this, however, your plants will need more nutrients during high summer. Water-in fertilizer (p. 51–52), or cover with a good inch of grass clippings. At the same time, cut and remove leaves that are starting to look ugly and rough.

**Weeds** are your biggest problem. As plants remain in the same spot for several years, weeds such as ground elder, creeping bellflower, and other bad guys have time to get a foothold. Always be ready with your hoe!

**Water!** Drought makes leaves less juicy. An alternative to watering is to keep the ground mulched with garden waste. This reduces your need to water a great deal, and the soil becomes porous and fertile.

**Refresh your perennials.** Perennials benefit from being divided after a few years, even if they come back year after year. To do this, dig up the plant in the spring and split it into three or four sections. Transplant them in a new place with very good soil, or give them away to someone else for their garden. Dividing them every four years is usually enough.

Self-seeding perennials, such as sea kale, scallions, and sorrels are true gifts. The seeds germinate all over in springtime. Be careful to not pull up and throw away the treasured seedlings when you weed. Dig up the seedlings when they're big

*Rhubarb bleached under a bucket develops a fine flavor.*

enough to handle, and then pot them so they can keep growing.

## SPRING IN THE TUNNEL GREENHOUSE

Even the weakest spring sun can heat up a greenhouse and raise the soil's temperature by a few degrees. This means that you can start sowing a month earlier than in outdoor beds. But only sow cold weather plants, and start sowing them when the soil temperature is at least 41°F (5°C). Preferably cover them with a row cover if the nights are still a bit chilly.

I sow spinach, arugula, radish, and other quick-growing things. My aim is to harvest these once it's time to put out tomatoes, cucumbers, and bell peppers, otherwise I risk running into a scheduling conflict. This isn't necessarily a catastrophe, however, since I then harvest the leaves while they are still tender.

You can also sow spring crops so they don't crowd the tomato plants but end up somewhere in-between, like a type of interplanting. This ensures that you'll definitely enjoy a nice harvest. I sow parsley and leaf lettuce, which take longer to develop, along the outer edges so they're out of the way.

If you don't plan to fill your greenhouse with tomatoes and cucumbers, you can grow whichever vegetables that take your fancy. Personally, I find it wasteful to grow kale and chard in a Mediterranean climate.

Tunnel greenhouses and other unheated greenhouses are also excellent for forcing plants. Here I see exemplary cabbages, fennel bulbs, cucumbers, squashes, and other plants. By all means, sow in cell pack kits. Thin so you get one plant per hole. The seedlings don't need to be potted up; just lift them out and plant them outside when it's time. Those of us who are in a hurry can even force lettuce plants so we can plant them outside early. They turn out wonderful.

Leave the air vents open slightly when the sun shines, but close them at night. If you can't check in every day, you'll have to make sure that one vent or other opening remains constantly ajar.

Be aware that slugs will find their way in; I really don't understand how. As soon as you spot holes in the leaves, it's time to go on the hunt, looking first under the leafy mass.

In the south of Sweden, tomatoes are often set out in late spring. Others wait until early summer.

## POTTING TIPS

- Get ample planters with draining holes in the bottom. Leafy plants don't need a lot of depth but they do need plenty of room around them. If they don't get this, the harvest will be very small.

- Fill the pots with planting soil. It's even better if you amend it with ⅕ of sifted compost. Preferably mix in some composted animal manure following the instructions on the packaging.
- Sow directly, or put in seedlings. Direct sowing is for when you sow directly outside, or a few weeks earlier. Cover with plastic or row covers and keep the plantings damp.

- Tomato and chili plants cannot be moved outside until nighttime temperatures are around 50°F to 53.6°F (10°C–12°C). But they must be hardened off, i.e., they must gradually acclimatize to life outdoors. Place them in the shade for a week. Be prepared to protect them with garden fabric or plastic bubble wrap if a cold snap hits.

- Perennial herbs sold at this time can be planted outside right away. They can tolerate frost.

| Minimum depth for planters. | |
|---|---|
| **PLANT** | **MINIMUM DEPTH** |
| Dill, cilantro, mâche, arugula | 4³/₄" (12 cm) |
| Mizuna cabbage, spinach, leaf lettuce, radish, parsley | 6" (15 cm) |
| Chard, early beets, carrots, kale | 7⁴/₅" (20 cm) |
| Potatoes, sweet peas, indeterminate green beans, squash, chili peppers, tomatoes | 9⁴/₅" (25 cm) |

**My Tunnel Greenhouse in April.**

Cos/romaine lettuce Little Gem

Cilantro

Signet Marigold

Onion, sets

Turnip (as border)

Parsley (as border)

Leaf lettuce (as border)

Arugula

Radish

Garden cress

Spinach

Mâche—winter lettuce—lamb's lettuce (as border)

Tomatoes and cucumbers will have to wait a little while we first grow spinach, lettuce, and arugula in the tunnel.
Next spread [80–81]: We harvest lots of spinach between spring and summer.

# SUMMER GARDENING

**THE BEST TIME FOR WARM WEATHER PLANTS IS HERE. THIS IS WHEN TOMATOES, CHILI PEPPERS, AND BASIL GROW AND FLOURISH. THE VEGETATION WE SOWED IN SPRING KEEPS ON DELIVERING, TOO. WHAT A PLEASURE, AND SUCH ABUNDANCE! BUT DON'T PUT AWAY THOSE SEED PACKETS YET, PLEASE!**

EVERYTHING IS SO SIMPLE in summer. Plants are sturdy and don't need to be coddled like newborns. Vegetables choke out the weeds, and we're kept busy harvesting!

High summer is also the time of the year when gardening is in sync throughout the entire country; it's summer in the north as well as in the south. Naturally, temperatures are higher in the southern county of Skåne than in northern Norrbotten. But the North's many hours of sun partly compensate for its lower temperatures.

Summer is just as much about planting as it is about harvesting and watering. We sow and fill gaps created by harvesting spinach, early carrots and potatoes, lettuce and radishes....We also sow plants for late fall's harvest, and, who knows, maybe even for winter's, too.

It's annoying, though, that seeds are taken off the shelf sometimes as early as mid-June. What's especially irritating is that shops remove seeds that should be sown in late summer and in early fall—I'm thinking of Asian cabbage plants in particular. We have to do what people have always done in times of rationing—we must hoard.

*No ifs or buts about it—tomatoes are the centerpiece.*

## GROW WARM WEATHER PLANTS

Some summers are really too short for many warm weather plants. That's why we start many of them indoors. In the north, sometimes you need a greenhouse. But if you live in the north and don't mind taking a chance, go for it! We need brave gardeners who go against the grain and who develop new gardening methods. And, who knows, the summer may turn out long and hot.

You can always buy plants if you don't have time to start them indoors. Unfortunately, plant nurseries don't always cater to vegetable gardeners, and you run the risk of ending up with poor quality plants. Here is my advice if you're buying plants:

Bigger is not always best. For that reason, refrain from buying tomato and chili plants that are overloaded with ripe fruit. They're going to have a rough time acclimating to their far tougher life outside. Go for plants with flowers and small unripe fruit instead.

Also, don't buy cucumber, squash, pumpkin, or cabbage plants that are overgrown and droop over the pot's edge. They'll barely survive being planted outside. No—plants must be small and plump.

The general rules for growing warm weather plants are this: The site should be sunny and

*The first artichokes are harvested in July. Old-fashioned sweetpea blooms are at the front.*

*We're inundated with all types of cucumbers during warm summers.*

preferably sheltered from the wind; and the soil needs to be porous and rich in nutrients. In short, the plants must bask in the warmth.

Following is a selection of our favorite warm weather plants. They can be a bit awkward to grow outdoors in a garden bed, pallet rim/raised bed, or in a pot, so I'm sharing my most import-ant tips here. You'll find information about sowing in the cheat sheet on p. 14 and in the pre-cultivation section starting on p. 62.

## CHECKLIST FOR THE SUMMER

Everything happens at once in summer: caring for spring plantings, harvesting of early crops, and then sowing again. It sounds like a lot work, but what's so good about summer is that there are very few "musts." It's not a big deal if you miss a fertilizing or a watering. The plants have

such an amount of built-in strength that they will survive some occasional neglect. Here is a checklist you can go through when you have the time and inclination.

**Loosen up the soil** if it is compacted and hard on the surface. You don't have to do this if you mulch.

**Fill up on nutrients.** Water in some fertilizer every other week, or every week if growth is lagging (see p. 51–52). Or, cover the ground with fresh grass clippings. Remember that legumes, root vegeta-ble, and potatoes don't need extra fertilizer.

**Stake up** cucumbers, tomatoes, broad beans, and other plants when they start touching the ground. Wooden poles and twine is enough.

**Planting warm weather plants outdoors.**

| PLANT | PLANTING OUTDOORS |
|---|---|
| Eggplant | In the south of Sweden you can grow eggplant in a pot placed outdoors in a sunny spot and protected from wind. But don't move the pot outdoors until nighttime temperatures are at least 59°F (15°C). I often get very good-looking fruits in a 12-quart (12 liters) bucket on the balcony, but I also grow them in a tunnel greenhouse. The yield is rubbish if summer is poor, but is quite satisfactory if the season is warm. Take note that lice and white flies take a shine to eggplant. This issue is usually resolved when you move the pots outside. If not, treat the plant with soapy water.<br><br>   Harvest the fruits before they're fully grown, as this will stimulate the plant to produce more fruit. Fruits that are left on the plant for too long easily turn woody. Select early-ripening varieties. |
| Basil | Don't move basil outside until nighttime temperature reach at least 53.6°F (12°C). Grow it in wide planters, basins, and crates, and leave a 2" (5 cm) space between the plants. This way you'll get a sea of basil, but you must water-in fertilizer weekly, just like with potted plants. In the south of Sweden you can grow basil in beds, but row covers are a must. Harvest it in consecutive batches to prevent the basil from bolting. |
| Chili pepper/bell pepper | Chili peppers grow surprisingly well in garden beds in the south of Sweden, as long as they're planted in a warm site that's sheltered from wind, and that you use a row cover. But the plants cannot be moved outdoors until nighttime temperatures are at least 53.6°F (12°C). Chilies require big pots—10 quarts (10 liters) or more. Varieties bearing smaller fruit are fine in smaller pots. Water with fertilizer each week or every other week. Lice are a big problem at the seedling stage. Rinse with lukewarm water and squash the egg clusters found on the underside of the leaves. If this doesn't help, you can spray with soapy water; mix 1-3/4 fl. oz. liquid soap in 1 quart lukewarm water. Harvest the fruits in consecutive batches to stimulate the plant into growing more fruit. You can harvest the fruit when it is unripe—green and yellow in color—or ripe fruits, which oftentimes are red. |
| Cucumber | Plant cucumbers outdoors when there's no more risk of frost. Grow them in a mounded bed, and preferably mix some compost in to the bed. Cover it with a row cover, and remove it once the cucumber begins to flower. Don't skimp on watering, because drought will make the cucumber taste bitter. Cucumbers grown in beds don't need to be tied, but they will be exposed to more light if they are. Harvest the cucumbers often, preferably once a day or every other day, and while they're young. If they're left too long on the vine they'll become more seed warehouse than fruit. Traditional cucumber varieties have both male and female flowers. The modern *parthenocarpic* varieties grow female flowers only and develop fruit without pollination. If they are pollinated, the fruit will become bitter and grow misshapen. This means you should not grow traditional cucumbers alongside modern varieties. |
| Artichoke | Plant outdoors when the risk of frost is past. The plants become big and bulky, and they devour nutrients. Besides soil-building fertilizer, this plant requires repeated watered-in fertilizing through the summer. A layer of grass clippings is a good alternative. One of the most important things to remember is to not ignore the distance between plants (see p. 18). Artichokes become infested with lice; fight them with the water hose and use strong pressure. If this doesn't work, use a soap spray (1 3/4 fl. oz. liquid soap per quart of lukewarm water). |
| Tomato | They need a sunny spot sheltered from wind. Don't move the plants outdoors until nighttime temperatures are at least 46.4°F–50°F (8°C–10°C). Plant them so the lowest leaves hover just above the soil, then pinch off those leaves. Tall (indeterminate) tomatoes need support while growing; it might be enough to just tie the plant to a stick. They also need pinching, which means that the side shoots that grow between the branches (see photo on p. 88) must be pruned off. If you don't pinch off those shoots, the plant will grow more competing stems. |
| PLANTING OUTDOORS | Determinate varieties can grow without support, but it's a good idea to tie them up when the branches start lying along the ground. You might also need to trim them a little to let in more sunlight for the fruit. Water in some fertilizer a few times during the growing season. You won't need to do this if you cover the soil with fresh grass clippings. Regularly remove leaves that have turned yellow or look like they've been attacked. It doesn't hurt a lush plant to remove the lower branches—in fact, it allows the fruit to receive more light. |

**Indeterminate tomatoes or bush (determinate) tomatoes?**

| TYPE | HEIGHT | PLANT LOCATION | GROWTH PATTERN | YIELD | FLAVOR |
|------|--------|----------------|----------------|-------|--------|
| Tall (indeterminate) | 5' to 6½' (150–200 cm) | All thrive in greenhouses, but they can be grown in outdoor beds in the south of Sweden. Stupice and Tigrella are special outdoor bed varieties. | Only one stem is allowed to develop. It gets tied to a tall support structure. Side shoots need to be pinched. | Very good yield if the summer is warm. | Here you'll experience a burst of flavor. Tastiest are the cherry tomatoes. |
| Bush varieties (determinate) | 1' to 2' (30–60 cm) | Do well outdoors, except furthest to the north. | They're allowed to branch out. Very bushy plants might require support and trim. No need to pinch. | Yield is a bit less than for indeterminate varieties, but they're early and grow fruit even when summers are cold. | Not quite as flavorful as indeterminate varieties, but still extremely tasty. |

However, pumpkin and squash can lie directly on the ground, preferably with a plank of wood placed under the fruit, which reduces the risk of spoilage and slug bites. You can never provide too much plant support—even summer flowers tend to tip over, and so they require staking.

**Both field and Spanish/killer slugs** are highly active. Water the plants in the morning so they're dry by evening. Take a tour of the garden in the morning and at night, and hunt for Spanish slugs. Chop them in half with a spade, a pair of scissors, or other sharp implement; you can then leave them on the ground.

**Keep an eye out for cabbage moths.** When white moths flutter around in the garden, it's time to inspect the undersides of cabbage leaves. White moths mean that cabbage butterflies and cabbage moths have probably started laying their eggs. Cabbage butterflies' larvae are green and measure about 1½" (3½ cm) long; cabbage moths' larvae are also green but are only ⅓" (1 cm) long. Both pierce cabbage plants with their gnawing. Sow beans now if you haven't had the time so far, or if the weather didn't allow it. The soil must be at least 53.6°F (12°C). Help the sprouting along by soaking the beans in water overnight.

**Water** before the soil dries up completely. Using a sprinkler system isn't very smart because it mostly wets the leaves. This in turn promotes fungal diseases and attracts slugs. It's better to water manually or get a drip irrigation hose that you can place between the rows.

**Check the carrots.** Black bite marks usually signal an attack by carrot flies. It's better to harvest carrots while they're small, rather than once they're large and heavily damaged.

**Mound the potato plants** by adding soil so the tubers aren't exposed to light. In the sun they will turn green and become inedible. Preferably, mound them with soil twice.

**Prune out the spent summer flowers** as soon as

*Right: Warm weather plants that I like: pole beans Neckargold, chili Brazilian Starfish, tomato Romanesco Fiorentino, and the cucumber Arboga.*

*Pinch tomato plants throughout the summer, i.e., pick off the side shoots between the stalk and leaves.*

*The best tip: Sow seeds—here, land cress or yellow rocket—in candy boxes throughout the whole season.*

they're done blooming. This promotes more flower growth. But if you wish to save their seeds, leave the seed heads alone. Summer flowers also require fertilizing.

**Turn the compost** to make it decay faster. But you only need to dig the surface material. By all means, tip a pot of urine into the compost now and then. It provides nutrients and promotes quicker decomposition. If the compost is dry, water it.

**Take photos of you crops and plantings.** This will help you in spring when you're planning your garden.

### POTATO LATE BLIGHT FUNGUS IS ON THE RISE

Potato blight is a fungal disease that attacks the plants of the potato family; primarily the potato, but also tomatoes.

The disease has increased dramatically, partly because summers have become warmer, but also because Sweden is host to a new type of spore that overwinters in the soil. This spore spreads primarily through the air, from patch to patch, from region to region. Contamination spreads quickest during a warm and damp summer.

Potatoes are usually under attack by as early as July. The first signs are grayish-brown spots that spread on the leaves, after which the plant turns yellow and becomes dry and brown. The blight reaches the tubers, which develop brown rot and become inedible.

How do we stop it from spreading? Well, remove the foliage! That means that you cut off the leaves and throw them in the garbage (never in the compost pile). Do this as soon as you notice the brown spots starting to spread.

The tubers can then be left in the soil. They'll grow another 10 to 20 percent. When you dig them up, toss the remaining waste in the garbage. This is especially important with potatoes that have been afflicted.

Tomatoes are also often contaminated by this blight. It begins with the foliage showing brown spots, which then spread rapidly; within a few short weeks the entire plant is destroyed and the tomatoes turn brown and hard. Inedible! Once the rot has spread on the leaves, it's better to pick

*The potato's foliage is the first to be attacked by the potato late blight fungus, followed by the tomato's leaves and the tomatoes.*

everything, even the green tomatoes. Diseased tomato foliage and tomatoes go straight in the trash.

## STAGGERED SOWING AND PLANTING

Now the time has come, my friends, to start practicing forward planning. We'll sow for late summer's, fall's, and late fall's harvests. And we're not doing it just the once, but as soon as we have the time and feel the urge to bring out the seeds. This is what my sowing schedule looks like during the summer:

**I sow where there are gaps** after harvesting spinach, early potatoes, early carrots, and beets. However, I refrain from planting the slowest growers, such as parsnips, Brussels sprouts, and winter carrots. And you must fertilize, of course, before you sow, with, for example, composted animal or poultry manure. If you know that your watering habit is 100 percent reliable, you can skip the row covers. You can't imagine how quickly things grow at this time of the year; thinning plants out is still just as important as ever.

**I repeat-sow** if the first sowing of, say, carrots, beets, beans, or other vegetables left me unimpressed. It nearly always works much better on the second try. Beans, especially, often require a second sowing.

**I force plants as if they were on a conveyer belt.** Why on earth, you might wonder. I do this because there will be free patches of soil in a week or two, and then it's very nice to have a batch of plants ready and close at hand. I force most of them in propagation stations, but it works just as well in small pots.

**I use the candy container trick.** At this time of the year I sow leafy greens such as chard, common purslane, and lettuce in plastic candy containers that I get free from the grocery store. I fill them with planting soil, sow the seed, cover it with some soil, and then water the whole thing. The containers are placed under glass, plastic, or out in the open. As long as you keep the soil damp, it will literally grow like weeds. When I need new plants, I

*At the height of summer, I fill in spots with new cabbage seedlings. Tender kale in late fall is absolutely delicious!*

*I do consecutive sowing and planting, even on the Hügel bed. Now we're going to plant fennel.*

just put a finger in the container and lift them up. They quickly take to their new growing spot.

**I'm stingy when sowing rows.** I sow a row of some of the plants listed on the next page whenever there's some available space, occasionally in between rows. These plants are not meant to grow big, but are meant to be available when I need some plants for fill-ins—it's a good way to use up the last seeds in a packet.

**I fill the cold frame** with peat pellets and propagation kits if there is space.

**I make note to** plant kale and black kale in July. These are exceptionally fine specimens that you can, if you're lucky, harvest during part of the winter or all through winter. They will be even more tender than the kale you sowed in early spring.

## AIM FOR A LATE FALL HARVEST

Now the question is, when do we plant to ensure a late fall harvest? I've learned a method of planning ahead from American gardeners, that I've adapted to work for us here. The figures are approximate, but they've been very useful for me.

Thanks to this calculation, I can time sowing so the plants are big and strong when the fall frost hits. Big plants are always more cold hardy than smaller plants.

The fall factor takes into consideration that plants grow a great deal more slowly in late fall due to the cold and the decrease in daylight. The same calculation applies to cold frames, greenhouses, or tunnels. In those instances, however, the fall factor lasts two weeks instead of three.

Here are the four factors you need to be aware of before starting your calculation:

**1. The time it takes for a plant to fully develop (see the cheat sheet p. 14)**

**2. The duration of its harvest period.** For example, spinach and radishes are harvested for 2 weeks, mizuna cabbage for 4 weeks. If you're not sure of the time, count 3 weeks, which is average.

**3. The fall factor,** which according to the American model is 3 weeks. It's 2 weeks if you grow your plant under glass or plastic.

**4. The first fall frost**—check your local weather.

These are all the things you need to know in order to anticipate the latest date you can sow. Let's say you want to sow radishes. Grow time is 30 days. Add in their harvest period, which is 14 days, and the fall factor, which is 21 days in an outside bed. Total: 65 days.

This means that you have to sow the radishes 65 days before the first fall frost. In Östersund, for example, that's September 15. So you'll sow 65 days before September 15, i.e., July 12 at the latest. In Stockholm, we base our calculations on the first frost being around October 15. We count back 65 days to August 11, which is the last day for sowing a radish outdoors in Stockholm. In greenhouse tunnels and greenhouses you can sow a week later. This calculation applies to whether you sow in beds or sow for plants.

I must admit that I occasionally sow at the start of September. But that means the weather has been incredible and that I feel like taking a chance.

## ASIAN GREENS

There is a group of leafy vegetables that are fall vegetables by nature and are sown in late summer or early fall. I'm referring to Asian greens, especially pak choi (celery cabbage), Japanese mizuna cabbage, and mustard greens, all of which are stubbornly attempting to integrate themselves into Swedish kitchen gardens.

Twenty-one years ago I wrote a book about these green vegetables. I have honed my growing methods since then, but have also become more impressed by these plants' performance.

I specifically remember a visit in October to a community garden in Gäddvik, just outside Luleå, in the northern Swedish county of Norrbotten. It was bitterly cold and nighttime temperatures hovered around 19.4°F (-7°C) for several nights. But the garden beds were magnificent: They were packed with billowing, fresh, green mizuna cabbage and other Asian greens. What a surprise; it was such a splendid crop that it could very well rival any Chinese planting.

Naturally, the conditions were ideal, which they needed to be. The plants grew in sizable raised beds with porous soil. They had been given all the nutrients they required, with lots of compost and animal manure from the sheep that grazed in a field near the gardens.

If you want to see awe-inspiring crops of Asian greens in person, go visit the community gardens on the edge of our bigger towns. The Chinese, Thai, and Vietnamese communities almost always grow Asian greens.

*Asian greens are sown in late summer.*

## FAST GROWING ALL-PURPOSE VEGETABLES

The plants survive cold snaps down to 23°F to 17.6°F (-5°C to -8°C). They will look rather rough, but they regain all their freshness as soon as temperatures rise above freezing. However, they do not tolerate prolonged winter chills.

Their second greatest virtue is their rapid growth habit. The seeds typically germinate as quickly as in four to five days. They've completely developed by five or six weeks. Since they grow so quickly, you'll have time to do several consecutive sowings. In Stockholm, I plant the first lot at the beginning of July, and keep going all the way till September.

Asian greens have a slight cabbage-y flavor, and are juicy and crisp. Mustard greens are a bit special; they contain mustard oil and have a distinct peppery bite.

Both the leaves and the stalks are edible. They're like an all-purpose vegetable in Asian cuisine, and are included in everything. They're eaten raw in salads, cooked in soups and stews, quickly sauteed in stir-fries, and used as fillings for pies, dumplings, and lasagna. . . . They are extremely nutritious, and are number one on nutritional scientists' top ten lists for their nutritional content.

## BOLTING AND PESTS

That was the fun part. Now we must look at problems that definitely exist, and which can have some awful consequences. I advise you not to start growing these greens without knowing all about them.

The troubles are almost always due to bolting and/or pests. Most of us know that spinach and arugula occasionally flower (bolt) too early. They're not interested in producing leaves if they're sown in midsummer—they want to produce flowers. The same applies to Asian greens.

There are many reasons for bolting. Drought is one of them; extreme cold or heat is another; serious malnutrition is yet a third. The days' length is also a factor. It's preferable to sow these plants in late summer or early fall to avoid these problems

And then we have pests, the worst of which being the flea beetles that chew on and destroy the beautiful leaves in spring. Unfortunately these attacks have nothing if not increased, which is why I only grow these greens in the fall now. Cabbage butterflies and cabbage moths can also wreck these leaves, but they tend to prefer broccoli, cauliflower, and white cabbage. Another pirate is the slug, but it is not exclusive to Asian greens.

## GROWING TIPS FOR ASIAN GREENS

**Porous and nutrient-rich soil** is vital, as are even levels of humidity. It's especially important not to let the soil dry out.

**The main sowing** is done in late summer. The last sowing is in mid-July in the north of Sweden, while in the south you can sow up into September, especially if you grow under a row cover, in a greenhouse, or in a plastic tunnel. The best growth will be under a row cover. Spring sowing is occasionally successful, but it's still best if it's done in a tunnel or a cold greenhouse.

**Once the seeds have germinated** and the first pairs of leaves have appeared, go ahead and mulch with grass clippings. This will help keep the soil damp and porous. At the same time, thin out the plants so they touch but are not overcrowded.

If the turnip flea beetles are chewing on the leaves, sprinkle the plants with ash, rock dust, or lime. This will calm them down. Row covers stop cabbage butterflies, cabbage moths, and cabbage flies from laying their eggs, but they are only effective if there are no gaps in the weave.

A strong protection routine is a must to **fight slugs.** Check for them every day in the early morning or late in the evening. Water the plants only in the mornings. Find out more about how to fight slugs on p. 44.

**Harvest** your plants before they bloom. Pak choi forms a head that can be pulled up as a whole. Mizuna cabbage and mustard greens can be harvested in consecutive batches. Mizuna cabbage can continue being productive for several months if given extra nutrients. If a plant shows a tendency to bolt, pick it immediately.

## NOT EVERYTHING THRIVES IN THE HEAT

Cold weather plants weren't made for summer heat, which is why they're grown as winter vegetables in, say, India and the Middle East. Fortunately, cold weather plants don't mind high summer temperatures if they're watered during a drought. This applies to all plants, from beets and chard to kale and onions.

But there is a bunch of vegetables that hate the heat and which demand special care; I think you should skip a few of them during summer. Spinach is such a vegetable, for instance. When I sow spinach in May, its leaves become almost grotesquely large. If I plant it at the beginning of June, the harvest is about one-tenth of its normal yield, and the quality of it is rubbish. A totally wasted effort!

On the p. 97 I've listed cold weather plants that, due to a variety of reasons, experience problems in summer's high heat, and occasionally also with the length of the day.

Best sowing time for asian greens.

| VEGETABLE | SPRING | EARLY SUMMER | LATE SUMMER | FALL |
|---|---|---|---|---|
| Choy sum | | | X | X |
| Komatsuna—Japanese mustard green | X | | X | X |
| Mitzuna cabbage | X | | X | X |
| Pak choi—celery cabbage | X | | X | X |
| Mustard greens | | | X | X |
| Tatsoi | | | X | X |

*Pages 94–95: A Chinese darling—pak choi. The best for stir-fries.*

## GET NUTRIENTS WITH GREEN FERTILIZING

Let's say you don't have the stamina to sow/grow more vegetables, and your soil is just as tapped out as you are. Consider this option: Sow a catch—sometime called cover or secondary—crop.

This is a type of green fertilizing technique in which you sow crops for the purpose of capturing the nitrogen that remains in the soil after the harvest. As this crop decays, vegetables will reap the benefit of nutrients that would otherwise be lost. Furthermore, the soil doesn't do well when left bare—and so it doesn't have to be. I highly recommend this method!

I sow catch crops after harvesting, say, early potatoes, which is already in July. But they can also be sown at the beginning of August. Some suitable catch crops are blue phacelia, subterranean clover, Persian clover, crimson (Italian) clover, and buckwheat. Legumes and clover vegetation bind nitrogen (see the table to the right). This means that the soil absorbs nitrogen when the crop decomposes. Commercially you'll find mostly crop mixes, but they are excellent.

Don't count on plants becoming as large as when they're sown in spring. However, by late fall you'll have a green, luxurious mat, bursting with nutrition. The crop is worked back into the soil, roots and all. Come spring, most of it will have decomposed.

You don't have to sow the entire bed. If you have harvested one row, you can sow your cover crop there and let the other vegetables keep growing. By doing this, you've gained several things: You've boosted your soil's nutrients and improved its structure, you've raised its humus content, and the worms will love you.

### TIPS FOR GREEN FERTILIZING

**Spread the seeds** evenly over the surface, and then rake them into the topsoil, first in one direction

*To the left, spinach sown in late June, to the right spinach sown in early May.*

and then in the other. Sow the seeds closely, as this kills the weeds.

**Keep the sowed area damp,** and keep pulling the weeds if it looks like they're taking over.

**Cut or mow** the plants in late fall. When you do your fall digging, the foliage and roots are carried along. You can chop up the coarse stalks. Another way to do this is to chop up the plants and mulch the soil with them for the winter.

### KICK-START YOUR CUT-AND-COME-AGAIN PLANTS

The most generous and productive of leafy greens are the come-and-cut-again plants. There aren't that many, but wow, what delight we get from them! Chard, leaf lettuce, parsley,

**Cold weather plants that don't like heat.**

| DOESN'T LIKE HEAT | GROWING TIPS |
|---|---|
| Broccoli rabe | Grow only in light, partial shade, and damp soil. It's better to wait until late summer. |
| Turnip | Is most tender and mild if sown in spring. But will also do well if sown in late summer. |
| Lettuce (leaf, head, cos/romaine and iceberg) | The seeds will not germinate if nighttime temperatures are above 68°F (20°C), so make sure to sow on a cool night. Or do this: Sow in planting soil in a container such as a candy box, water, and place everything in the refrigerator for 48 hours. Then remove the container and put it outside. The seeds will germinate after a few days. Once the seedlings grow between 2" and 2¾" tall, plant them outside. Do it on an overcast day and cover with row cover. |
| Arugula | Will only grow in part shade and damp soil during high summer. The risk of bolting is high. Better to sow during late summer. |
| Radish | These can be sown year-round, but are tastiest if sown in spring. |
| Celery cabbage (pak choi), mizuna cabbage, and other Asian greens | Sow these in late summer or early fall. They prefer short days and reasonable warmth. One of our best fall crops. |
| Spinach | Hold back on sowing until late summer or early fall. Planting this at the beginning or in middle of summer is useless. |
| Mâche (winter lettuce) | Bolts easily in summer and the seeds don't germinate well. Wait until late summer or early fall. |

**Green fertilizer crops.**

| PLANT | GOOD FOR | HEIGHT |
|---|---|---|
| Crimson (Italian) clover | Nitrogen-binding plant with beautiful purple-red flowers. | 1'⅔ to 2'¼ (50 cm–70 cm) |
| Buckwheat | A strong grower that keeps the weeds down. Performs well even in compacted clay soil. | 2' to 2'⅔ (60 cm–80 cm) |
| Persian clover | Nitrogen-binding plant that's a strong grower. Its flowers smell very nice. | 2' to 2'⅔ (60 cm–80 cm) |
| Subterranean clover | A low, mat-forming nitrogen-binding clover plant. Very quick growing. | 10" to 7¾" (10 cm–20 cm) |
| Blue phacelia | Luxurious leafy mass with strong tap roots that break up the soil. If you're lucky, you'll have time to enjoy the blue lilac flowers that are very attractive to insects. Very quick growing. | 2' to 2'⅔ (60 cm–80 cm) |

wild arugula, mâche, buckhorn plantain, amaranth, and purslane—they grow almost non-stop throughout the summer.

However, they are very keen on bolting in high summer, in order to produce seeds. They're in even more of a hurry if there's a drought and a lack of nutrients. So why should we stop the flowering? Well, bolting prevents the leaves from growing and their taste becomes bitter and uninteresting.

There are three things you must do to restart leaf production. First, cut down the plant until only a few small leaves remain at the base. Then, break up the soil around the plant. Finally, fertilize the soil. This you do by watering in fertilizer (see p. 49–52) or by covering the soil with freshly cut grass clippings. You can also work in some animal manure.

The plant will now start to grow nice leaves again. If the plant persists in bolting, maybe it's time to say goodbye to the leaves and let the plant produce seeds instead. Or, simply dig up the plant.

Even perennial vegetables, can be kick-started this way at the height of summer. Read more about it on p. 72.

## SUMMER IN THE TUNNEL GREENHOUSE

Spinach, radishes, and other plants that you sowed in springtime and have now harvested have gobbled up most of the nutrients in the soil. This means it's time to fertilize again. Amend the soil with composted animal manure, or cover it with fresh grass clippings.

If you still have some warm weather plants on hand, it might not be too late to set them out in high summer; the condition is that you'll have to plant them in the greenhouse.

The new kid on the block—perennial kale—is new to me too, so I don't have an opinion on it yet. Plant it the same way you would sow it outside, and set tomato, chili, and bell pepper plants deeper than they were in the pots. Cucumbers, however, are planted at the same level as when they're potted.

You must plant smart so the plants get as much light as possible. Situate low plants at the front, and set tall specimens farthest at the back. Cucumber typically grows tallest and hogs most of the light.

The rate of growth will now go pretty crazy, and within a few weeks it'll be time to stake up tomatoes and cucumbers. Bamboo poles measuring 6 ½ feet (2 meters) are good for indeterminate tomatoes. Even better still, let a piece of twine hang from the ceiling, a bit loosely at the beginning. As the tomato plant grows, wrap the plants' stalks carefully around the twine. Stake cucumber in the same way. I prop up determinate (bush) tomatoes, eggplants, paprika, and chili peppers with poles.

It gets way, way too hot when the sun is beating down. It can reach 104°F (40°C) in the

*Don't let the purslane bolt! Pinch off all its flower buds.*

*An abundance of cucumbers in the greenhouse: Above is the heritage variety Arboga Vit. To the right is a Chinese long, burp-less, cucumber.*

greenhouse, and plants don't like that. It's best to put up a shade cloth, at least on the sunnier side. An old lace curtain works also. But first of all, open all the doors and airing vents; everything must be ajar when the sun shines. You can close them at night, but you can also leave them open.

Check at even intervals that the corners of the planting bed don't dry out.

Continue to force plants. They will grow even better if you place their propagation trays in the greenhouse.

### POTTING TIPS

• The nutrients found in commercial soil are already spent at the end of three weeks. Fertilize now with liquid organic fertilizer or with pellets of poultry manure. But best is still gold water. Use a ratio of 3 ⅓ fl. oz. urine to 9 parts water—a purer fertilizer does not exist.

• Set out tomatoes and other warm weather plants if you haven't already done it. Stake up those that are already outside. Regularly trim off ugly, withered leaves.

• Prop up sun-loving plants. There's always a bit of shade behind tall plants, even on the sunniest of balconies. Rearrange the plants so the shortest ones are at the front. Why not place some on high stools or shelves in the background?

• Be prepared to water every single day. You need not water as often if you mulch with bark, grass clipping, stones, or cones from the forest floor. You must provide shade—with a parasol, for instance—if you are away from home for a few days.

• Break up the surface soil now and then; this is a good way to check that the roots aren't drying out in the pot. If there is room for more soil, add some to the pot in late summer.

• If you have a spare pot, plant another crop of leafy greens. Mizuna cabbage is a fall favorite on the balcony, just like the red-veined leaf lettuce. Direct sow and cover with plastic.

| To Sow for Late Fall Harvest. |
| --- |
| Head lettuce |
| Kale |
| Mizuna cabbage |
| Chard |
| Leaf lettuce |
| Wild arugula, wild rocket |
| Pak choi (celery cabbage) |
| Spinach |
| Black kale |
| Watercress |
| Common purslane |
| Mâche (outer edge) |

| In My Tunnel Greenhouse in July. |
| --- |
| Eggplant |
| Chili peppers and bell peppers |
| Chinese long cucumbers |
| Hungarian peppers |
| Indeterminate tomatoes |
| Signet marigolds |
| Italian parsley (along outer edges) |
| Spinach |
| Black kale |
| Watercress |
| Purslane |
| Mâche (along outer edges) |

*My balcony edibles in high summer. Here the tomatoes are always healthy and sweet tasting.*
*Pages 102–103: No kitchen garden should be without summer flowers, which attract beneficial insects.*

# FALL GARDENING

**LEAVES ARE TURNING YELLOW AND WE'RE REACHING FOR A SWEATER. HOWEVER, THIS DOESN'T MEAN THE SEASON IS OVER. AND IT'S GREAT THAT THERE ARE SEVERAL VEGETABLES THAT ARE AT THEIR FLAVOR PEAK AFTER A TOUCH OF FROST.**

In my area, meteorological fall begins at the end of September. However, I already feel fall approaching at the start of the month. Evenings are cooler; the air is crisper; and the community garden is more or less empty. One neighbor after another packs up their things, leaving only a few die-hards behind. It's a pity because of the mild fall sun, and because of all the Italian radicchio. Not to mention the kale, which the cold has mellowed to a fine flavor. I fill my harvest basket easily.

Many warm weather plants are starting to wither now, or have already done so. One exception is the rocoto pepper (*Capsicum pubescens*), also called the manzano pepper. It's surprising in its cold hardiness, and it can usually handle a few hard frosts.

## FOUR FALL BEDS

If you visit my garden in the fall, you'll notice four things. First, garden beds are covered with garden vegetation waste. I do this so the soil doesn't stay bare through the winter, and because I know from experience how crumbly and nice the soil will be come spring. My mulch is made up of leaves, straw, pulled weeds, and other vegetation waste.

Second, you'll find one or two green-fertilized beds; the mats are primarily blue (or lacy) phacelia and Persian clover, sowed in late summer. Occasionally the entire bed is green fertilized, but more often than not one or two rows of vegetables are still lagging in the same bed.

The third thing you'll notice is kale, salsify, leeks, parsnips, radicchio, chard, watercress, and other cold weather plants that grow well into late fall, and which can all cope in a few degrees below freezing. A few of them might even get the opportunity to overwinter.

I'm just as pleased each time that I allowed them to spread.

But the fourth and most interesting things are the plants I sowed sometimes in late July or August. That's when I carried out forward planning, and I'm now reaping the harvest from that strategy. The Asian greens such mizuna cabbage, mustard greens, and pak choi (celery cabbage) especially love the fall. I'm not exaggerating when I say that the bed is bursting with growing power.

Land cress and buckhorn plantain are two other rascals that can also occasionally be found

*Left: In August, we harvest tomatoes, Hungarian peppers, and root vegetables. Pak choi seedlings are growing in the propagation tray.*

*Green fertilizer plants have created a green carpet. Underneath the buckets we're bleaching radicchio Castelfranco.*

*Top: Some beds are mulched as early as September. Bottom: The watercress is left to spread out in the cold frame.*

among the fall greens. The first grows slower than Asian greens, but has the advantage of tolerating a few more degrees below freezing. Heads up, however, for those with palates that are more sensitive: winter cress tastes like watercress but has ten times more bitterness and bite. Buckhorn plantains, which also don't mind some degrees below freezing, are much kinder in flavor. I love its nutty taste; it's just right for whatever salad mix you have going! Both plants are harvested in consecutive batches. Here, that means a good spell into winter.

## TIME TO GET THE ROW COVERS OUT AGAIN

It's a bit of a pain to haul the row covers out again, but I advise you to do this, especially if you want to harvest long into fall and even a little in winter. It's time to cover up once nighttime temperatures hover around 41°F (5°C).

The cover may not increase the temperature much more than a single degree, but it becomes very snug and warm under the cover once the sun shines. The cover protects against the wind, which in turn safeguards against the cold. The windchill effect is more significant than we

*End of October in the mobile growing tunnel: chard, kale, and radicchio.*

imagine; the cooler it is outside, the colder the windchill. For example, let's say that it's 32°F (0°C) outside, but the wind blows at 14 meters (16 yards) per second. The effective temperature—how cold it really feels—is 5°F (-15°C).

If I compare vegetables that have grown under row covers with those that grew without shelter, the former always win. They're both more attractive and tastier. They occasionally grow a little, even if the light is weak.

Don't forget to secure the material properly so a fall storm doesn't blow the cover off. Covers also protect against deer, but not 100 percent. If it snows, you must of course shake the snow off, otherwise the plants won't get any light.

Slugs remain a problem. It's easy to forget about them once the cover is back on and we're into late fall. Thankfully, their ravenous appetite ebbs as temperatures fall. But keep in mind that Spanish slugs are active down to 46.4°F (8°C). Field slugs are even tougher and can be active at just above freezing.

## MOBILE TUNNELS ARE A FAVORITE

Growing tunnels complement row covers. Tunnels are in fact better, because they're encased in plastic, which protects more effectively against the wind than fabric. Also, woven covers become extremely brittle when they freeze. Personally, I'm extremely pleased with my mo-

*Vegetables of the future: all kinds of kale—smooth, curly, green, yellow, and red.*

Windchill factor. The table illustrates actual temperature at different wind speeds (in meters per second). SOURCE: SMHI.

| | 50°F (10°C) | 42.8°F (6°C) | 32°F (0°C) | 21.2°F (-6°C) | 14°F (-10°C) |
|---|---|---|---|---|---|
| 2 m/s | 48.2°F (9°C) | 41°F (5°C) | 28.4°F (-2°C) | 15.8°F (-9°C) | 6.8°F (-14°C) |
| 6 m/s | 44.6°F (7°C) | 35.6°F (2°C) | 23°F (-5°C) | 8.6°F (-13°C) | 0.4°F (-18°C) |
| 10 m/s | 42.8°F (6°C) | 33.5°F (1°C) | 19.4°F (-7°C) | 5°F (-15°C) | -4°F (-20°C) |
| 14 m/s | 42.8°F (6C) | 32°F (0°C) | 17.6°F (-8°C) | 3.2°F (-16°C) | -7.6°F (-22°C) |
| 18 m/s | 41°F (5°C) | 28.4°F (-1°C) | 15.8°F (-9°C) | 1.4°F (-17°C) | -9.4°F (-23°C) |

bile growing tunnel. I usually place it where vegetables, such as parsley, chard, beets, and mâche that might survive a few degrees below freezing, are already growing. It's a few degrees warmer inside the tunnel, according to the digital thermometer.

The chard, especially, looks fantastic, and it's a real treat to harvest chard until right before Christmas.

It's very important that the soil be porous, regardless of how and where you garden in late fall. The soil cannot be dry or wet—just damp. The worst soils are dry and sandy, or hard, wet clay.

Growth has often ceased by late fall. Because of this you usually won't need to fertilize. Only add nutrients if you know that no fertilizing was done in late summer.

If so, then you can water in some fertilizer.

As for choosing a site for your tunnel, remember that the sun hangs quite low in late fall, so choose a very sunny spot.

## THE FALL FROST ATTACKS

With a hard frost, we can get a taste of winter several weeks before it's finally here. In the morning, leaves are covered by a shimmering weave of ice crystals. It's just as beautiful as it can be damaging. Most warm weather plants can't handle any frost at all if they're not adequately sheltered.

Norrland—in the north of Sweden—is one of the areas most affected by frost; so is the northwest of Svealand; the South Swedish Highlands; the area of Kolmården; and the inner parts of the island of Gotland. The south and west coasts fare best; likewise the areas around the big lakes Vänern and Vättern.

Fall frost hits primarily at night when the weather is clear, the wind is calm, and the temperature sits just below 32°F (0°C). Ice crystals—frozen damp air—form on horizontal surfaces, like leaves. In the insert to the left you'll find the average dates for the first hard frost. But count on there being variations. Furthermore, temperature differences can be significant, even within the same area—yes, even in the same garden. Low-lying areas are the first to be affected.

A few years ago, growers at Järvafältet, on the outskirts of Stockholm, were surprised by a catastrophic hard frost at the beginning of September. I had planned a visit there to photograph their glorious community gardens, but instead came face to face with beds in which squash, cucumbers, and pumpkins lay like flaccid dishrags on the soil. In my own garden beds, one Swedish mile away, I didn't see a hint of frost until two months later.

## START A FROST WATCH

So what can you do ahead of time to prevent frost from killing your garden? Forward planning applies here, as does a frost watch. Keep a watchful eye on the thermometer and on online weather sites.

Frost watches begin about two weeks before the average date of the first frost. For Stockholm, that's October 15. This means that I start my frost watch at the changeover from September to October. I'll begin even earlier if the air is especially nippy and the weather is clear. I'll check the thermometer every evening and take a peek at the excellent weather site smhi.se or yr.no.

Everything is fine and dandy if it's 46.4°F (8°C) or warmer in the evening. The probability of a hard frost striking is minimal and I'll get a good night's sleep.

I'll cover my warm weather vegetables—tomatoes, peppers, cucumbers, squashes, and pumpkins—with row covers if the thermometer dips lower than 46.4°F (8°C). The fabric raises the temperature by a few degrees, which is usually enough to carry the plants through the first light frost, i.e., just below freezing for a few hours. However, you can't be sure that it'll be enough to protect from several hours of hard frost.

By contrast, frost is not fatal to cold weather

*An early frost and the pumpkin should be inside. Hopefully the frost didn't damage the fruit.*

plants. It can even improve their flavor, which I will tell you more about in a moment. But it doesn't hurt to cover the plants anyway, especially if the temperatures creep down to below 41°F (5°C). Growth will also be faster under a cover.

Does it sound like pain to have to keep an eye on temperatures throughout fall? Don't worry, you'll get used to it, and it might even add a bit of excitement to your gardening. Also, don't forget that a hard nip of frost can be followed by a few weeks of high summer heat. Plants might experience a few more great weeks of sun and growth if you can shelter them from frost damage.

## THESE PLANTS TASTE BETTER AFTER A COLD SNAP

I wish you could perform a side-by-side taste test of soups made from kale harvested in July and from kale harvested in November. The positive impact of the frost would be obvious: The November kale is mellower and sweeter. Its bitter aftertaste that many don't care for disappears with the frost.

*Kale enjoys a good frost, and gets even tastier. Its bitter bite mellows while its sweetness increases.*

**111**

| Different kinds of frost | | |
|---|---|---|
| | **DEGREES** | **EFFECT** |
| Light frost | 30.2°F to 28.4°F (-1°C to -2°C) for a few hours | Damages unprotected warm weather plants such as pumpkins, cucumbers, and tomatoes. Chili peppers might survive. |
| Hard frost | 28.4°F to 24.8°F (-2°C to -4°C) | Most cold weather plants will tolerate 24.8°F (-2°C), but not everything will cope with 24.8°F (-4°C). Even perennial leaves might get damaged. |
| Killing frost | Colder than 24.8°F (-4°C) for several hours. | Most plants will become severely damaged or die. |

The flavor of many other vegetables is enhanced with a touch of frost. So why harvest them before frost?

In the table on the right-hand side, I've listed specimens whose flavor is perfected thanks to a nip of frost. Of course, this is only possible if they haven't suffered past hardship such as drought and insufficient nutrients. No frost in the world can work wonders against the bitter taste and bad flavor that stems from this type of treatment.

So what's the reason for this change in flavor? Well, plants fight for their lives; they know that they're facing a death threat and so they grab the only weapon they at their disposal—they raise the sugar content of their structures. They do this by converting carbohydrates to sugar.

When sugar is dissolved in water the freezing point is lowered, so the plant can take a few more degrees below freezing. As a result, it kills two birds with one stone: It tolerates a harder frost, and it gets better tasting to boot. But eventually this sugar boosting strategy stops working, so of course the plant dies.

*Savoy cabbage tolerates harder frost than red, white, and pointy cabbages. Vorbote is the name of this variety.*

## THE ITALIANS REACT

As you've seen, the cabbage family is most favored by frost. Another important group is the Italian lettuces of the chicory family. These include lettuce such as sugarloaf, red endive, and radicchio Castelfranco; also included are escarole and frisée.

All these plants have a natural bitterness that Swedes seldom appreciate. But after a frost, this bitter flavor changes and sweetness takes the lead. What is left is a piquant snap of bitter, and a delicious crispness that is a fit for hearty salads.

To please the Italian lettuces, escarole, and radicchio Castelfranco, they should not merely feel a nip of frost but also be bleached. A few weeks before you expect to harvest the plant, tip a bucket over it. A few air holes in the bucket are necessary; you can also leave a gap between the soil and the bucket.

| Tastier after frost. |
|---|
| Mustard greens |
| Brussels sprouts |
| Escarole/frisée |
| Kale |
| Jerusalem artichokes |
| Kohlrabi |
| Carrot (late variety) |
| Parsnips |
| Leeks |
| Sugarloaf lettuce |
| Celeriac |
| Belgian endive |
| Red Russian kale |
| Black cabbage, black kale |
| Mâche |
| White and red cabbage |

I'm sure I've missed a few vegetables when compiling the list of those that improve with a touch of frost, so you will have to keep up the research. This is a topic you can learn more about. In the end, you'll be so picky that when in the produce aisle, you'll ask if the cabbage was harvested before or after a frost.

Then we have vegetables that taste better after they've been stored for a while. Winter squash is a great example—pumpkins from *Cucurbita maxima* can be stored until spring. You can also eat them directly after harvest, but their flavor will be less developed.

*The Italian radicchio Castelfranco turns into a refined vegetable when it's bleached under a bucket.*

*The Italians grow Piennolo tomatoes, a variety that keeps for a few months at room temperature.*

And why not try Piennolo tomatoes? This is a special variety of tomato with thick skin and a pointy end. In Italy they're referred to as everlasting tomatoes. Heavy bunches, called piennoli, are hung at room temperature and can stay there until late winter. I won't say that a Piennolo tomato tastes better than a sun-ripened cherry tomato harvested in August, but it definitely gets tastier than when it was just harvested. It doesn't matter if the Piennolo hasn't had time to ripen when you harvest. Even the Italians will occasionally harvest them unripe, because they will ripen as they are suspended. Principe Borghese is a Piennolo variety that is indeterminate and easy to grow.

## GROW YOUR OWN SEEDS

You'll save lots of money by becoming your own seed supplier, and those seeds usually germinate faster than commercial ones. You can try it with summer flowers such as tagetes (marigolds), ca-

lendula, and Indian cress if you're just starting out…it's ridiculously simple. As soon as the seed heads feel dry and start to crumble, pick them and bring them inside.

Peas and beans of all kinds are about the easiest. You let the pods stay on the plant as long as possible. Inside, the bean and pea seeds are ripe when the pods start to become dry and turn brown.

Chili peppers are straightforward, too. Just rake out the seeds from the ripe fruits—same for tomatoes. However, tomato seeds tend to be wet and messy, so place them in a glass of water and stir them now and then. The debris will float to the top in a few days, at which point you can strain it off. At the bottom of the glass you'll have clean seeds that you now can dry on sheets of newspaper.

So far, everything has been unfussy because I haven't mentioned the risk of cross-pollination. To gauge this possibility, you'll need to know if the plant is cross-pollinating or self-pollinating (see the cheat sheet on p. 14). Cross-pollinator flowers, like those of squash plants, are fertilized by pollen from other flowers through insect activity and wind. If several varieties grow side by side, cross-pollination will occur.

Because I'm crazy about Costata Romanesco squash, I want to collect seeds for that variety of squash only, and not some weird mix resulting from cross-pollination.

Professional seed producers keep a safe distance of about 550 yards (500 meters) or more between plants. Since that's a challenge for most hobby gardeners, the solution is to only grow a single variety the year you're growing squash for seeds.

Then you have self-pollinators, which are fertilized by pollen from their own flowers. You can grow several types of self-pollinators, but it's preferable to keep a distance of about several yards (meters) between them. If you're unlucky, an insect might interfere with pollination and cause cross-pollination.

You can also loosely wrap the budding flower—in a big bag made of woven fabric, for instance. Remove the bag as soon as the fruit begins to develop, that way you can be sure that the variety is true to type.

Many believe that seeds need to be replaced each year, but that's only true for onion seeds and parsnips. Other seeds can keep for two, three years, or more. In practical terms this means that, for example, I don't have to collect broad bean seeds every year. I gather them every four years, and only grow one variety at a time. If I wish to grow a tomato for its seeds, I pot it and make sure it's not too close to other varieties of tomato when it begins to flower.

I've only covered annual plants here. If you'd like to grow biannual vegetables like beets, cabbage, and carrots for seed, their roots need to

overwinter first. If you want to tackle this job, I suggest you read up on the subject and become familiar with it (see p. 119).

### TIPS FOR GROWING FOR SEED

**Pamper vegetables** that are going to produce seeds. Thin them so they have twice the amount of room as other plants. Apply extra fertilizer and water them often.

**Grow one variety at a time** if the plant is a cross-pollinator. As most seeds remain viable for several years, you don't have to grow this particular plant for seed until a few years from now.

**Opt for the nicest** and most representative examples. You yourself get to decide which qualities you want to put first. Early maturation is important if you live in the north of Sweden. Of these, go for the earliest plants. For lettuce, spinach, and other leafy greens, it's important that they flower as late as possible. In this case you'll want the plants that flower last.

**Grow several plants for seed,** preferably five or more of each variety. That's the only way to ensure that all parental qualities show up in their seeds.

**Let seeds mature** on the plant to the point that they almost drop off the plant, and harvest them in dry weather conditions. You'll often end up collecting them in successive batches, as not all seeds mature at the same time. If there's an early frost or if it looks like the seeds might rot in the fall rain, bring the plant inside. Let the seeds ripen and dry out inside where it's airy, preferably hung upside down with a newspaper placed underneath.

**Clean the seeds.** If the seeds are still inside their pods, shells, and capsules, crush them. Blow off

or sift out the debris afterwards. You can also remove the debris by winnowing, i.e., shaking the seeds and the debris until they separate, which they will do. Then it's easy to blow away or brush off the debris afterwards. Dry the seeds for a few more days after cleaning them, just to be on the safe side.

**Vegetable-fruit** such as tomatoes, bell peppers, cucumbers, and squash can be left on the plants until they're ripe—overripe, even. The seeds inside will not be ready until then.

**Store seeds in a dry and dark place** during winter. Peas and beans are best kept in paper bags, while other seeds do better in airtight bags. If you wish to extend the viability of the seeds, wrap them tightly in plastic and keep them in the freezer.

**Go for safe bets.** Here are some good choices: broad beans, peas, chili peppers, tomatoes, dill, Indian cress, lettuces, and summer flowers.

## BUILD A HÜGEL BED

One of the most useful activities in the fall is to build a Hügel bed, which is a cross between a compost pile and raised bed. It's certainly packed with garden waste, but it differs from straight composting in that the bed is watered frequently and basks in sunlight. That's why things grow so exceptionally fast in the bed, and waste breaks down into friable soil in only one season.

The bed warms up quickly in the spring because it's significantly elevated. As it decays it also generates a certain amount of heat. There

*Left: Seed harvest: Different types of chili pepper are ready to be threshed, as well as beans, pumpkin, and squash.*

*Homegrown seeds appreciate folded homemade paper bags.*

are plenty of nutrients available for plants, which are released gradually. No wonder things grow so well in it!

Occasionally I've grown pumpkins in a conventional raised bed next to a Hügel bed of comparable size also containing pumpkins. The Hügel bed ends up producing twice as many pumpkins.

The bed is built on the principle "higher is better." You start off with small twigs and you end with partially broken down compost and soil. Some animal manure is very effective in a Hügel bed, not only because it fertilizes but also because raises its temperature. Fresh grass clippings have the same effect.

By year two, the Hügel bed will have sunk some, but it's still a great growing site. You can also use the soil as compost.

A Hügel bed not only produces superior harvests, it also makes fantastic soil amendment. If you choose a new site each year for your Hügel bed, you'll soon turn the worst, can't-do-anything-with-it soil into a superb, loamy soil.

*There is no better site for squash and pumpkins than in a Hügel bed in full sun.*

The bed builder might run into trouble now and then in early summer as the layer of soil won't be thick enough, at which point growth stops and the leaves turn yellow. So it's a good idea to start by sowing spinach, radish, arugula, or other leafy greens with shallow root systems. Once they're harvested, it's time to plant out cucumber, tomatoes, squash plants, and other heat seekers. By then the soil will have broken down and there'll be enough room for their larger root systems.

The instructions below are for a temporary Hügel bed. Maybe you'll only grow on it for one season only and then spread out the soil. However, if you want a permanent bed that you can grow in over several years in a row, place larger wood logs and other tree waste in the middle of the bottom layer as a foundation. This will maintain the bed's humidity, add stability, and help you get rid of wood waste. In Germany, this is called Hügel cultivation.

## HOW TO BUILD THE BED

**Start in the fall** when there's plenty of garden waste available. If you start in the spring you'll need to get going as early as possible so decay is properly underway when it's time to sow or plant.

**Situate** the bed in a sunny area and set its alignment north to south. This way the bed is exposed to the sun on both sides. The width should be 4' to 4 ¼' (120–130 cm). The length of the bed is up to you. Its height should be approximately 3 ¼' (100 cm).

**Remove grass sod** and other growth. Place the clumps and pieces of sod to the side in a pile. They'll soon come in handy.

**Build a wooden edge,** or set timber on the bed's long sides. This will stop the soil from washing away. Now we're ready to build the bed.

**The first layer:** Approximately 1 ½ ft. of branches from berry bushes and trees. Cut or chip the branches to a size not longer than 8" to 12" (20–30 cm). Spread over a few buckets of topsoil or compost soil. Remember to do this between each layer of waste.

**The second layer:** 8" (20 cm) of heavy, coarse garden waste. Here you can put in the clumps of sod that you dug up earlier. Place the sod upside-down. Cabbage stalks and the coarse stems of Jerusalem artichokes and sunflowers are good here, too. It's best to chop it all into smaller pieces with a spade.

**The third layer:** 8" (20 cm) fine garden waste, primarily grass clippings, pulled weeds, and leaves. If you have access to animal manure, mix some into this layer.

**The fourth layer:** 4" (10 cm) of partially decayed compost. Use garden soil if you don't have any compost.

**The fifth layer:** ⅓ to ½ ft. (10–15 cm) of garden soil or planting soil (½ ft. (15 cm) if you're building the bed in spring. Heads up! Don't use only planting soil as top layer! You must mix in some composted soil and/or garden soil.

**Tamp down** the top of the bed when it's ready to make a flat surface. This will help it retain water. If you make the bed in winter, cover it with black plastic or winter mulch it with some straw and/or leaves.

## FALL SOWING

Before you quit your gardening activities in the fall, I suggest you give thought to fall sowing. A review of garden books from the nineteenth century and even earlier reveals that fall sowing was a no-brainer. This habit, like many other sensible cultivation habits from that era, has been largely forgotten. But it seems that a renaissance may be underway.

Fall sowing is not to provide you with a bigger harvest. (Whether it does or not is a subject we will come back to later on.) No, its purpose is to yield an earlier harvest. Early sowing means you avoid infestations of early pest insects like willow-carrot aphids. It's also pretty wonderful to have a garden bed all ready and sown when the frozen ground thaws. And you save time because seeds sown in the fall germinate earlier. They're so battered by water, snow, freezing, and thawing that the seed cover has softened. Then, when the soil's temperature is optimal and the sun is shining brightly, the seeds are in the starting blocks and set to germinate immediately.

Expect seeds to appear more thinly in the rows, so it's a good idea to sow them a little close.

However, one main problem is that fall sowing won't work in compacted, clay soil. Wet clay lies like a cement lid over the row, and the seeds either will not be strong enough to push through

### MAKE A HÜGEL BED

A cross section of a Hügel bed shows coarse garden waste at the bottom and finer garden waste further up. Soil covers the top layer.

Leaves, pulled weeds, animal manure, compost soil

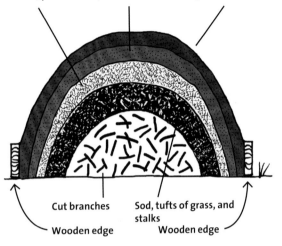

Cut branches    Sod, tufts of grass, and stalks
Wooden edge    Wooden edge

or they will rot. If you wish to sow in the fall in clay soil, cover the row with sand.

### PLANTS FOR FALL SOWING

You'll find crops suited to fall sowing among the cold weather plants. You'll get the most out of slow-growing specimens. Those first coming to mind are parsnips, parsley, and carrot.

My personal theory, however, is that everything that self-seeds in the garden is good for fall sowing. A self-seeding habit is obviously proof that the seeds benefit from lying and resting in the cold winter soil. In my garden, those would be seeds for leaf lettuce, parsnip, and marigold.

Otherwise, my ideal garden bed for fall sowing includes a row of parsnips, one of parsley, and one of carrots, all of which have a long, drawn-out starting time in the spring.

You can also fall sow arugula and garden cress, of course. But since they grow extremely fast, I don't see the point of doing this.

Some report success with fall sowing beets. If you want to try this, you'll need to sow them in light soil on southern and southwestern slopes.

### FALL SOWING THROUGHOUT THE COUNTRY

Fall sowing should take place as late as possible in the season, but before a hard frost sets in the ground. Seeds are not meant to start growing in the early fall. If there's already hard frost you can still sow. Scratch a furrow in the ground and sow in it, then cover the seeds with soil mixed with sand, or sand only.

Before you sow in fall, you'll need to remove all perennial weeds, otherwise it'll be impossible for you to work the soil in spring. Fertilize before you sow; this is the only time that vegetables are fertilized in fall.

The end of September is usually a good time for fall sowing in the north of Sweden; the end of October is good in the middle of the country; in the south, fall sowing is done at the end of November.

### TIPS FOR FALL SOWING

- Fall sow in only one garden bed or pallet rim/ raised bed.
- Sow the seeds a little more closely than usual.
- It's better to sow too late than too early.
- Go for the slowest growing seed varieties.
- Sow in loose soil, and by all means cover the sown row with soil mixed with sand.
- Cover with a row cover in the spring.

## IT'S TIME FOR GARLIC

I've now finished sowing in my garden beds. However, garlic—or, more correctly garlic cloves—must be planted in the ground in the fall if you want a good harvest in time for summer.

The farther south you live the later you can plant your garlic, preferably at the end of October. Up north, we'll plant it a month earlier. If you put garlic in too early, it might rot.

I recommend that you buy garlic cloves from certified seed, which are guaranteed to be disease-free. Otherwise you might run the risk of contaminating your crop with diseases like, among other things, white mold (rot). I ended up with garlic riddled with white rot when I bought it at a market in Estonia. Lesson learned. White riot by itself is extremely difficult to get rid of.

Plant the cloves 2 ⅓" (6 cm) deep, root end down, the pointy top facing up; leave a distance of 6" (15 cm) between the cloves, and a row distance of 7 ¾" to 9 ¾" (20 cm to 25 cm). Garlic needs deep and fertile soil. Occasionally it has time to sprout and green up a little in the fall, but otherwise it does this in early spring.

You can snip off a small amount of the green sprout, the emphasis being on "small." The leaves turn yellow in July, which means that the small clove has become a sturdy head of garlic made up of several cloves. It's time to harvest.

Savor the smell of the newly harvested onions! Don't they have the most irresistible aroma? That's the proof in the pudding that homegrown and store-bought produce belong to two different worlds. The same holds true for fresh garlic flavor.

And remember—don't wait too long to harvest garlic. If you do, the cover that keeps the cloves together will burst, and the garlic will lose its phenomenal storing quality.

## FALL GARDENING: TUNNEL GREENHOUSES

Now, inspect the tomato plants still producing. Pick off all leaves that seem afflicted with potato

*The germination rate for seeds sown in the fall is a bit lower, but we solve this by sowing closer together.*

late blight fungus (see p. 88). Also, nip off all discolored leaves at the bottom. It's good to let light and air in between the branches.

Even cucumbers, bell peppers, chili peppers, and melons benefit from removal of ugly leaves. They might be attacked by disease-causing organisms and also hog daylight.

The more diligently you harvest, the quicker the plant will produce again. So, harvest often and repeatedly. As you know, tomatoes continue to ripen in a sunny window. Cucumbers and chili peppers are tasty, even if they're small.

As soon as you've freed up space in the tunnel, decide what to do next. Here are options:

**Mulch** the soil with leaves, straw, or other vegetative waste. This is the simplest option, and it pays off in better soil in the spring.

**Fall sow a bed** according to the model on p. 118 to get to see an extra-early harvest in the spring.

**A cold/hot frame** in the greenhouse will produce a harvest as early as in February. Prepare the frame site by putting down lots of mulch so the soil doesn't freeze when you install it, which won't happen until in late winter.

**Aim for a third harvest.** This assumes that you have forced plants. I usually have seedlings of kale, black cabbage, mizuna cabbage, pak choi (celery cabbage), leaf lettuce, and winter purslane (miner's lettuce). Work through the soil and fertilize it before you plant. A bit of compost is perfect here.

**Bet on a fall harvest!** You can take a chance and sow some very quick-growing leafy greens such as garden cress, spinach, and arugula. I can't promise anything, but who says plants must always be full-sized? Occasionally, some days can be blisteringly hot even in the fall, so leave the greenhouse doors open on sunny days. However, doors and vents should be closed at night. It's especially important that everything be closed if strong winds are in the forecast, or else your greenhouse can inflate like a balloon and tear apart. Use row covers if nighttime temperatures are below 41°F (5°C).

*It's best to buy garlic cloves from certified seed.*

## TIPS FOR POTTED PLANTS!

- Need more nourishment? The pots are empty of all nutrients by now. Water in fertilizer weekly.
- Place the pots along walls of the house. The plants need more sun, more heat, and more protection against the wind.
- You won't discover dry roots until you've dug down into the soil a bit. Then you'll also see if the soil is root-bound. If that's the case, cut off a piece of the root mass and add fresh soil.
- Do the chili peppers have a hangdog look about them? If so, move them inside and place them in a sunny window! But do leave them outside for as long as possible, as this is best for them and they can tolerate a lot more than you think.
- Once the plants are past flowering and producing, empty the contents into garden beds and other plantings. They can also go into a garden compost pile, but not into kitchen compost.
- Perennial herbs and plants that are meant to overwinter tolerate the climatic conditions better if they're dug down—pot and all—in, say, a garden bed.

*Right: I'll cover with row covers when nighttime temperatures are 41°F (5°C) or colder in the tunnel greenhouse.*

# WINTER GARDENING

## WINTER GARDENING IS BOTH EASY AND HARD, BUT I HAVE FOUND A MODEL THAT WORKS. BE PREPARED: THIS GARDENING WILL TAKE PLACE INSIDE.

Ever since I saw the winter garden beds in northern China, about fifteen years ago, I've wondered why we don't do something similar here. I've dreamed of being a winter gardener. Those beds were so deeply settled into the soil that they were almost like graves. They faced south to absorb maximum sunlight, and they were covered by construction-grade plastic or glass. On cold nights, they were also covered with warming mats.

Asian greens such as pak choi (celery cabbage), tatsoi cabbage (spinach mustard), and Chinese cabbage are grown in these types of beds. All these greens tolerate a few degrees below freezing. Here the temperatures were higher and more even, and the crops were protected from the wind.

My eyes were also opened a few years ago to winter gardening in the northern US and Canada. I saw pictures of lush vegetables that were harvested and grown in the midst of the bitterly cold winter, even at temperatures we're familiar with in northern Sweden.

So I thought, if the Chinese and the Canadians can do it, so can we. I had already begun to experiment with prolonging the growing sea-

*Left: Bah, a bit of snow on the black cabbage won't hurt it.*

son, both in spring and in late fall, with positive results. But gardening in winter was something new—and what a challenge!

### AT LEAST TEN HOURS OF DAYLIGHT

I followed the American and Canadian recipe to the letter: All the plants I grew were cold hardy (see the cheat sheet on p. 14). I sowed early enough to ensure that the plants had established a good root system by October. No tiny plants here.

In October, beginning of November—no problems. But then the plants began to lose their freshness and so also their flavor. After a while, many of the plants just laid down and gave up. And I'm not talking about kale and parsnip, which can survive most winters, but about regular cold weather plants like chard, arugula, and spinach. And once the plants lose their flavor, I lose interest in them.

Keep in mind that my observations relate to the area around Stockholm. Farther to the south, December can also yield a small harvest. However, it's not realistic to expect November harvests up north.

But why doesn't growing work as well in my area in Sweden as it does in North America, Canada, and northern China? They too go through bitterly cold winters and snow. There is a very simple explanation for this: the light, or more precisely, the lack of light.

Temperature isn't the only inhibiting factor in winter gardening. Access to daylight is another one. Plants need at least ten hours of daylight to grow. Photosynthesis doesn't happen if they get any less.

Daylight length depends on the latitude we live at. Stockholm is on the 59th latitude, whereas Beijing is on the 40th latitude, as is Madrid in Spain and Ankara in Turkey. It means that in January, Beijing, in China, sees over three hours more daylight than Stockholm. This makes a difference. The Northern United States and Canada also get a few more hours of winter daylight than we do. Eliot Coleman, who introduced winter gardening to the US, lives in Maine, which is on the same latitude as Bologna in Italy.

That fall in Sweden is typically miserable, dreary, and gray doesn't help matters. Weeks can go by without a hint of sun. Indeed, we lack both daylight and sunshine.

The table on p. 128 shows the amount of daylight hours in different areas of Sweden, in October through February. You'll notice that even within this country there are important differences. However, we as a whole get less than ten daylight hours per day between November and February.

## SO YOU STILL WANT TO GARDEN IN WINTER?

Even though the above reading material isn't exactly encouraging, but it doesn't mean that a winter harvest is out of the question. Not if you live in southern Sweden, and not if you choose the cold hardiest plants—those I call winter plants. These are cold weather plants that can tolerate 10.4°F (-12 °C) or colder. They can't be grown in winter up north, but they can certainly help ensure a prolonged fall harvest.

The information table on p. 128 lists these tough plants and tells how many degrees below freezing they can handle. But how well they hold up doesn't just depend on the temperature—these plants will give up earlier if there is recurrent freezing and thawing. However, a bit of snow has no detrimental effect on them.

There are borderline cases, plants that are almost winter crops; this includes black kale, cold hardy leek varieties, and celery. My experience is that they are hardy a little while into winter, but not much longer past that.

We can't do anything about the lack of daylight, but we can affect temperature by growing winter plants in a plastic tunnel, for example. Why not use a movable tunnel that you can shift easily (see p. 33)? The plastic will raise the temperature and offer protection from the wind. You can harvest Jerusalem artichokes and parsnips in the middle of winter if you've covered the ground to prevent the frost from permeating the soil. By the way, this applies to all root crops that are still in the ground.

I suggest that you use a heated cold frame (also called hotbed or hot box) if you want to be sure of reaping a harvest in February or March. This method yields a lot of vegetables in late winter and their quality is superb. It's also a lot of fun, even though it does require hard work. Of course we have another option at our disposal, which is to grow indoors. It doesn't yield the same quantities as a garden bed, but it does provide equal delight. We'll talk more about this in the section on indoor gardening.

## GROW AND HARVEST IN A HEATED FRAME

We're now in February, and everything on the gardening front is looking cheerless except in the kitchen window. But those who set up a hot-

*Right: Straw bales insulate well. But I forgot to scrape the snow off the windows.*

| PLANT | TOLERATES DOWN TO | TIPS |
|---|---|---|
| Brussels sprouts | 10.4°F (-12°C) | Protect against wildlife. |
| Kale | -0.4°F (-18°C) | Protect against wildlife. |
| Purple salsify | -0.4°F (-18°C) | Can be harvested throughout winter if you cover the soil to prevent it from freezing. Cover with straw, mats, bubble wrap, plastic tarp, etc. |
| Jerusalem artichoke | -0.4°F (-18°C) | Can be harvested throughout winter if you cover to prevent the soil from freezing. See above tip on how to cover. |
| Chard, green | 10.4°F (-12°C) | Preferably cover with plastic or row cover. |
| Parsnip | -0.4°F (-18°C) | Can be harvested throughout winter if you cover the soil to prevent it from freezing. |
| Parsley | -0.4°F (-18°C) | Keep it preferably under plastic or row cover. |
| Radicchio Castelfranco | 10.4°F (-12°C) | Cover with a wooden box or a bucket. Keep an eye on them over winter and harvest the leaves that start to wilt. |
| Buckhorn plantain | -0.4°F (-18°C) | Preferably keep under plastic or row cover. |
| Scorzonera | 3.2°F (-16°C) | Cover the soil to prevent it from freezing. |
| American/land cress | 10.4°F (-12°C) | By all means, grow it in a plastic tunnel, as it has a tendency to become too peppery or sharp in flavor otherwise. |
| Miner's lettuce | -0.4°F (-18°C) | Preferably under plastic or row cover. |
| Mâche | -0.4°F (-18°C) | Preferably under plastic or row cover. |

**Plants referred to as winter plants that can tolerate at least 10.4°F (-12°C). SOURCE: VIRGINIA STATE UNIVERSITY.**

bed in the winter have much to look forward to. This method is a voracious consumer of animal

*Miner's lettuce is a little-known toughie that survives in -0.4°F (-18°C).*

manure, and it involves plenty of hard work. I'm not lying when I say that pushing wheelbarrows full of manure through 1 ½ foot (½ meter) high piles of snow is back breaking work. However, you are rewarded with crisp lettuce leaves in mid-winter.

Using hotbeds is an ancient gardening technique. Anders Lundström, one of Sweden's foremost expert gardeners of the nineteenth century, explains the purpose of the hotbed like this:

"During a season when the climate of Nordic Countries puts nature into a deathlike rest, when snow covers the ground and the cold transforms the mighty rivers into icy slides, you can still, with such simple materials as a covering of straw litter and livestock manure, defy climate's violence.

*Jerusalem artichokes can be harvested throughout winter, but mulch the ground so the soil doesn't freeze.*

*Winter may not be a threat to kale, but you must protect it from deer, hares, and rabbits.*

Make use of the livestock droppings and the properties of glass to trap heat from the sun's weak rays, and force them to rouse the slumbering life force within the seed. This way we can provide for the household's early vegetable needs."*

But it's in mid-nineteenth century Paris, France, not Sweden, that we find in the most impressive examples of hotbeds. What were called market gardens (*la culture maraichère*) occupied one-sixth of the town's surface—talk about community gardening—and they were extremely productive. Everything was grown in hotbeds over winter. There were smoking hot frames as far as the eye could see—there must have been thousands of them. Parisians had, thanks to this method, all their vegetable needs taken care of year-round. They exported cucumbers to England in the winter. Cucumbers in January? The

English were astounded and envious. In time, they copied their method.

### HOW A HOTBED WORKS

A hotbed's source of energy consists of horse manure combined with straw. This mix is called a litter bed. Its temperature rises as early as a few days after the litter bed is made. It lets us know that the decomposition has begun—that the microorganisms in the manure are hard at work. There are billions of them in the bed, and when they're at their most efficient the temperature rises to around 149°F–158°F (65°C–70°C). Then the heat levels off and falls to about 68°F–86°F (20°C–30°C). In the best case, the hotbed will remain at that temperature for several months. During this time, we can grow in the bed even if outside temperatures are freezing. For

*Handbok i trädgårdsskötseln, 1841* [ A gardening manual, 1841. *Swedish only*]

*It's better to prepare your hotbed in the fall. A pit is dug and filled with straw and/or leaves.*

*At the beginning of February: It's almost boiling in the hotbed. Sowing is done when the temperature has fallen to 59°F to 68°F (15°C–20°C).*

this to occur, however, the bed must be sunk deep and be protected outside with additional litter.

I visited a communal garden group not long ago, and they had a different way of doing things. Instead of using animal manure they added kitchen waste, which they collected from a local after-school facility. The waste was mixed with leaves to form a type of litter. They added about 7 ¾" of soil on top. Waste and leaves heated the crops, which were planted in double pallet rims. The pallet rims were then placed in a tunnel greenhouse.

The disadvantage of kitchen waste is that doesn't generate a lot of heat. The waste might also attract rats. Old garden books also mention kitchen waste as an option, but it's usually mixed with manure to make it heat up more.

## LITTER BED AND TEMPERATURE

In Sweden, hotbeds are pressed into service primarily between February and April—April is when we start to get sufficient daylight. How long into spring we can keep the heat up in the hotbed depends on several factors.

One is the litter bed's depth: The deeper the bed, the higher the temperature, and so the longer the heat will last. A litter bed prepared in January needs to be 2 to 2 ¾ feet (60 cm–80 cm) deep. A depth of 1 to 2 feet (30 cm–60 cm) is plenty if the litter bed is put together in March.

Of course, temperature is also tied to what type of manure you're using. Fresh horse manure is best—we could even say it's ideal. Heat production starts quickly and continues over a long period. Horse manure older than six weeks has probably already started to break down and so generates less heat. Fresh manure is light colored, whereas old, ripe manure is dark brown. Cow manure is also good, but it doesn't heat up quite as much as horse manure.

Your choice of litter is just as important. A classic litter bed contains one part fresh animal manure to two parts straw. Some stables use peat as litter, and that's okay but you will need to add an equal amount of straw. Dry leaves can be substituted for straw, even if they don't generate quite as much heat as straw. A good mixture is half straw, half leaves. The more manure in proportion to the straw, the warmer the hotbed, and the quicker the heat will be used up.

*Middle of February: The hotbed is sown and has begun to germinate. We air it out for a while every day.*

However, it's mostly geography that will have a direct impact on when you start and when you finish. In the north of Sweden you start in March rather than in February, because daylight is still too weak in February.

### EVERYTHING THAT YOU'LL NEED

**Horse manure** is easy to find; call your local riding stables. Make sure they don't use wood chips as litter because that won't work.

**Straw and/or leaves.** Try to find bales of straw. Check online and call local farmers. You'll collect and store leaves in the fall and dry them out over winter.

**Lumber for a wood frame/raised bed** (see measurements in next column). Pallet rims work, even if they are a bit on the small side. You'll need a window identically sized to the wooden frame. If you don't have a window, tightly wrap some plastic over a frame with the same outer measurements as the raised bed.

**Loose garden soil** preferably amended with some composted soil. If you don't have any thawed soil, buy some bagged soil.

**A digital thermometer.** It will stay permanently in the bed.

**Something to keep it warm.** Use rugs, straw mats, or anything similar that can be placed on the hotbed during cold nights.

### HOW TO MAKE A HOTBED

**1. Prepare the hotbed** as early as fall by digging a 1 to 1 ½ foot (30 cm–50 cm) deep ditch, and fill it with straw, hay, or anything that will prevent the base from frosting. The soil that you've dug up can be placed in a pile next to the hole. The ditch's measurements should be equal to the size of the hotbed, plus another 1 foot (30 cm) all around. Fill the hole with straw, hay, or whatever else that will stop the bottom from freezing. If drainage is an issue (or if you're unable to dig), place your insulation directly on the ground.

**2. Get material.** Start early, because collecting materials is usually what takes the most time. Check the list (at left) for all the required supplies and tips on how to acquire them.

**3. The raised bed frame** you're growing in must be 4' wide (120 cm) and about 8" (a couple of decimeters) deep. Suitable (untreated) wood dimensions are 1" × 7 ¾". Let the raised bed angle toward the south, either by building it 4" (10 cm) higher on the back side, or by placing the bed so that it tilts toward the south.

**4. Add in the litter bed** a few weeks before you wish to start cultivating. Start by emptying the ditch you dug of all the straw and stuff inside. Then fill it with one part animal manure and two parts

## HOW TO BUILD A HOTBED

The temperature inside the hotbed stays at around 68°F (20°C), even on a winter's day.

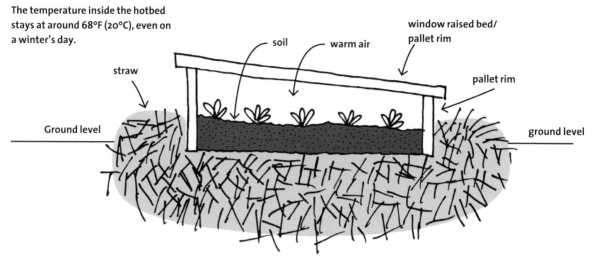

straw until the litter bed is as high as you want it. Mix it thoroughly and tamp down the bed with the back of the shovel. Water it if the contents are dry. (It won't hurt to empty the chamber pot in here.) Now, place the raised bed frame over the bed litter. Add in a few wheelbarrow loads of litter, both inside and outside the raised bed frame, and stir. You'll need one part leaves to three parts animal manure if you use leaves only.

**5. Insulate from the outside.** You now have about 1' (30 cm) or more of litter that will heat up from the outside. Unfortunately, straw blows away easily, so if you're feeling ambitious, build a frame that will hold in the litter. If not, just stomp down on the litter with your rubber boots.

**6. Keep an eye on the heat.** The temperature will probably rise to 158°F (70°C) now. Turn the bed once again, and remember to mix the material from the edges in with the material from the middle. Tamp down on the material and even it out with the shovel. After a few more days the temperature will begin to fall. When it's around 122°F

(50°C) you'll add the planting soil into the hotbed. It's great if you can amend it with some compost soil. For leafy plants, a soil depth of about 4" (10 cm) is fine—otherwise you'll need about 6" (15 cm). Finish by installing the window on top.

**7. Time to sow.** You can sow once the soil's temperature is around 59°C to 68°F (15°C to 20°C). Row distance in the hotbed should be about 7" (18 cm). A distance of 2 ¾" (7 cm) is plenty around the outer edge. A good trick is to alternate between quick and slower growing plants, like this for example: leaf lettuce, radish, early carrots, arugula, turnip, spinach, and mâche. First harvest the radish, arugula, and spinach. Your second harvest will be a few weeks later. Water so the soil doesn't dry out, as this would have catastrophic consequences.

**8. Once the seeds are growing,** they demand a lot of light. Don't let the temperature exceed 86°F (30°C)—plants don't like it too hot and will become lanky, especially if it's overcast and gray outside. Lower the temperature by opening the window.

**9. Air it out** a little every day by propping a wedge between the window and the frame. Leave it in place the entire day if the sun is beating down, but close it as soon as the sun disappears behind the clouds, and add some protective insulation for the night. Temperatures can reach over 86°F (30°C) in the hotbed in the spring, at which point you can remove the window for the day.

**10. After the harvest.** When the heat is spent and you have finished your harvest, spring is here. Now you can use the hotbed as a cold frame, because this kind of frame is excellent for forcing plants. Yes, you can grow vegetables in here, too—the spring sun is out now.

**11. You can repurpose the used litter** to mulch the vegetable bed. If you compost the litter, it can be used as soil in the hotbed next year.

## WINTER GARDENING IN A TUNNEL GREENHOUSE

Hopefully one of the beds is fully, or at least partially, filled with some of the plants I just described as winter plants. When temperatures dip down toward freezing, it's time to add extra covers to the tunnel greenhouse. This means you cover the plants with row covers. But don't do this if temperatures go over 41°F (5°C), because the fabric steals some of the daylight. The colder it is outside, the more degrees you'll gain inside by using a cover. The remaining beds benefit from being covered by leaves, for example.

### TIPS FOR POTTED PLANTS

- Occasionally, clay pots will crack in the winter cold. Place them in a frost-free area if you wish to protect them.

- Chili pepper plants that have been moved inside are usually covered in lice at this time of the year. It won't be enough to spray them once with soapy water (1 ¾ fl. oz. of liquid soap per quart lukewarm water); you'll have to repeat the process several times.

- Cut down the chili plants in late winter (February–March) to make them grow full and nice. The sunnier the window, the earlier you can trim them. Also, repot them in new soil.

## INDOOR GARDENING

No one was against indoor gardening as much as I was. A few years ago, an editor at one of Sweden's largest dailies called me for some advice on indoor gardening. I quickly brushed aside the request, declaring that indoor gardening was, and would always be, totally pointless.

Despite my long-held bias, I have English garden guru and author Marco Diacono to thank, because he got me to try out something I thought was useless. I was in the audience at a garden show in England where Marco was clowning around onstage, showing us a piece of metallic gutter which, according to him, would revolutionize the kitchen.

Cilantro sprouted in the soil-filled piece of metal. According to Marco, the plant's flavor was concentrated in the budding greenery. He circulated it around the audience, which duly inhaled its scent and sighed with delight. According to Marco, this budding greenery was 40 times more nourishing than its larger leafed counterpart.

| OUTDOOR TEMPS | INSIDE UNCOV-ERED TUNNEL GREENHOUSE | INSIDE TUNNEL GREENHOUSE WITH ROW COVER FABRIC |
|---|---|---|
| -16.6°F (-27°C) | 3.2°F (-16°C) | 17.6°F (-8°C) |
| 0.4°F (-18°C) | 10.4°F (112°C) | 24.8°F (-4°C) |
| 17.6°F (-8°C) | 24.8°F (-4°C) | 35.6°F (2°C) |

SOURCE: *FOUR-SEASON HARVEST*, ELIOT COLEMAN.

*December–February: Snow has bedded down the garden, so now we're gardening indoors.*

*January salad with indoor grown microgreens: amaranth, pak choi, pea, and sunflower shoots.*

The source for this statement is research undertaken in Maryland, in the US. Scientists checked the content of vitamin C, carotenoids, and a list of other substances in sprouting leaves, also known as microgreens. The results indicate that microgreens contain higher levels of vitamins and other phytochemicals than fully developed plants.

Once at home, I realized that the gutter method was a bit inconvenient. Why drive to the home improvement store and purchase construction parts that I would then need to cut to size, when I already had plenty of useable containers in my kitchen? And so my experiments were off and running.

### HARVEST AFTER TWO WEEKS

You can garden indoors year-round, but I only do it in winter. That's when my longing for fresh greens is strong enough to make it worth my while. I grow on about 10 ¾ sq. ft. (1 sq. meter) and in a window. It certainly doesn't fill any big baskets, but whatever I end up with is fresh. It beats outdoor gardening in both proximity and speed. I can look forward to a small harvest in only two weeks' time.

However, there is a small snag, and again, it's the lack of adequate daylight. Photosynthesis doesn't happen if the light is too weak; the plant doesn't get any nourishment and cannot grow. Therefore, you might need artificial light, i.e., grow lights. You'll get all the information about choosing and using grow lights on p. 67.

I've tried to grow most plants indoors—well, apart from things that get too big, such as root vegetables, squash, and white cabbage. Other plants, like peas, I've given up on because the yield is minimal. The plant itself climbs and thrives, but the pods I get can be counted on one hand. The same goes for beans. This does not mean you can't grow them indoors. In fact, you can grow a whole bunch of other vegetables indoors over the winter months, but their output is poor.

In my experience, the following three win: Leaves, both seedlings and more or less mature plants; and herbs (annuals and perennials); and sprouts.

## MICROGREENS OR TENDER LEAVES

I make a distinction between microgreens and tender leaves. If I talk about watercress growing in the kitchen window, you'll know what I mean with the designation microgreens. Seeds are sown so closely together that they form a dense mat of sprouting plants that are harvested as soon as this mat is formed. The plants consist of the plants' first leaves, i.e., the cotyledons at the base and the pale stalks. Both the leaves and stalks are harvested and used.

If counted by volume and weight, microgreens don't provide much, but they do grow quickly. You can harvest them in about two weeks. If you have a really bright window, you don't even need a grow light. Microgreens act as a flavor enhancer and add zip to salads and sandwiches, a bit like sandwich cress.

Tender leaves are real leaves that are of the same size as those available in bulk, or bagged, in groceries stores. We can describe tender leaves as greens that haven't grown quite as densely as microgreens, and which have been fertilized and allowed to grow some more. The leaves are about 2 ¾" to 6", and they're perfect for salads and stir-fries. Tender leaves require a lot of light; they really need grow lights.

## THE WAR AGAINST FUNGUS GNATS

Damaging pests are not a major problem in the indoor cultivation. There are lice, but they're seldom on green leaves. If you find them, it's probably because they've wandered off a potted plant or maybe chili pepper plants. Crush them with your fingers, or better yet—harvest the leaves!

However, a rather bigger nuisance are fungus gnats, sometimes called flower flies, which you've probably seen flit across your field of vision. They've ruined many of my plantings. They lay their eggs in damp soil, and evil larvae measuring about 0.26" to 0.27" (6 to 7 mm) long emerge from the eggs and eat the roots of the tender seedlings, which in turn makes the plants flop over and die. Basil is the hardest hit, but lettuce is also a vulnerable target. Sturdier plants such as broccoli, radishes, peas, and fenugreek can typically withstand the onslaught. The larvae die in dry soil, but we don't want the soil to dry out because then the plants will die instead. You can fight gnats by attaching strips of glue to which they become stuck; this will decrease their numbers but won't eliminate them. There's an electronic trap that has proven quite effective. When this isn't enough, I'll buy small envelopes of nematodes, which I then water in. This is an organic method that works, but it's expensive.

Stay away from bagged soil that has been kept at above freezing temperature over winter. The flies could have multiplied in those bags, whether the bags were kept at home or stored at garden nurseries. The best way to store bagged soil is outside, so the soil freezes.

*You can grow in a room under grow lights. Here grow both microgreens and tender leaves.*

## THE MOST BUDGET-FRIENDLY SEEDS

Seeds sold for growing in the garden can also be used for indoor gardening. However, this can get expensive, especially if you're growing microgreens, which need to be sown very densely. I only use garden seeds if I have small dribs and drabs left in seed packets that I wish to get rid of. It's much more economical to buy bags of seeds that are meant specifically for microgreen gardening. They can also be used for tender, small leaves.

However, I often get my seeds from the health food store, which sells organic seed for sprouting. They're useful for both microgreens and tender leaves. If you can't find any in the store,

*This is how I harvest chia leaves: I lift up the green mat and cut off the microgreens.*

*It's fun to test new greenery. This is buckwheat, which I sprinkle over food or mix in a green smoothie.*

look online. You'll find plenty of sellers and choices.

Seeds sold for eating are also a good option, as long as they have not been shelled.

It's no exaggeration to say that there are hundreds of different plants to choose from. In the sidebar I've listed some that do very well both as microgreens and/or small leaves.

## SOIL OR PAPER TOWELS

I've tried to sow seeds on all types of possible and impossible substrates and surfaces, and in my opinion, soil or paper towels work best. In addition, they're good for composting afterwards.

I use a double layer of paper towels for seeds **for microgreens**, especially if the seeds are small like those of garden cress, arugula, and chia leaves. Remember that if you grow on paper towels, you must harvest them as microgreens; there aren't enough nutrients to sustain more growth. You can grow microgreens in soil. I always grow sunflower shoots and pea shoots in soil, and I let them reach about $\frac{1}{3}$" to $\frac{3}{4}$" tall.

For **small leaves** I always use soil, about $\frac{3}{4}$" to $2\frac{1}{3}$" deep. Basil usually gets the most soil because I want to grow big plants and do staggered harvests. I use KRAV-certified planting soil [KRAV

**138**

is a Swedish nonprofit certification indicating that a product is organic, free of pollutants and GMOs, and its collection has not harmed any ecosystem].

Garden soil is no good here, because it's far too compacted.

If you have really fine seeds that you want to pamper, go ahead and mix a quarter of perlite or vermiculite into the soil. Both are mined materials with a fantastic ability to fluff up the soil and prevent compaction. And fluffing is exactly what indoor gardens thrive on! But this is a luxury method!

## TROUGHS AND TRAYS

To start, we'll skip the usual plant pots. When we look at their comparatively small growing area, we notice that they'll require an unnecessary amount of soil relative to the small harvest they yield. Also, the seeds and seedlings are at increased risk of rotting when set in deep pots. What we need are shallow containers with a large diameter.

Use plant pallets, trays, kitchen containers, and, last but not least, Styrofoam and plastic trays from the grocery store. The latter are best because you can easily poke drainage holes in them. It is also practical to use narrow, rectangular containers if you're using a narrow windowsill to cultivate on. After all, we must match our containers to the growing site.

The bottom of the container must have drainage holes so excess water can run off. There are times when I don't want to pierce and ruin an attractive container. I simply tip the container regularly to drain off the water. It works. Peas and sunflower seeds are best at surviving an undrained container.

You can build shelves in the window if you're short on space. Or, why not turn an old storage shelf into an indoor gardening site? You can mount the grow lights underneath each shelf (see p. 69).

Plants that do well as microgreens and/or small leaves.

| PLANT | MICRO-GREENS | SMALL LEAVES |
|---|---|---|
| Amaranth | x | x |
| Basil | | x |
| Mustard greens | x | x |
| Buckwheat | x | |
| Broccoli | x | x |
| Chia | x | |
| Fennel | x | x |
| Chard | x | x |
| Mung bean | x | |
| Pak choi (or other Asian greens) | x | x |
| Parsley | | x |
| Leaf lettuce (preferably red) | | x |
| Corn (for popping) | x | |
| Cilantro | x | x |
| Arugula | | x |
| Radish | x | x |
| Red cabbage | x | x |
| Siberian (Russian) kale | | x |
| Garden cress | x | x |
| Sunflower shoots | x | |
| Spinach | | x |
| Miner's lettuce | | x |
| Mâche | | x |
| Garlic greens (garlic cloves) | | x |
| Pea shoots | x | x |

## HOW TO GROW MICROGREENS

**Line the bottom of the growing vessel,** which only needs to be ⅓" to ¾" (1 to 2 cm) deep, with a double layer of sturdy paper towels. Dampen the paper towels.

**Sow the seeds densely,** but not to the point they're on top of each other. You can sow larger seeds such as cilantro, radish, sunflower, and peas in soil to a depth of ¾" to just over 1" (2 to 3 cm). That way you can harvest them either as microgreens or true leaves. Water the seeds with a spray bottle.

**Cover the sown seeds** with plastic, plasticized fabric, or a damp towel, and let the seeds germinate at room temperature, or better yet at a slightly warmer temperature. Remove the cover and place the container under a grow light when the seeds start to grow.

It is critical to keep the soil damp throughout this whole process. You achieve this by misting water over the sowing with a spray bottle. However, you don't need to fertilize. The seeds' nutrients will suffice.

**Harvest** as soon as a lush green carpet of cotyledons appear. The simplest way to do this is to lift the mat and cut off the growth at the base. Harvest both the leaves and the stalks. If the leaves turn yellow, they're lacking in nutrients, so you'll need to harvest them ASAP.

### HOW TO GROW TENDER LEAVES

**Fill the growing container** with soil to a depth of 1 ⅓" to 2 ½" (3 to 6 cm), and water the soil. The deeper the soil, the bigger the leaves you can grow. Sow the seeds more sparsely than for microgreens—about ⅓" (1 cm) between seeds is good. Cover them with a thin layer of soil and water everything.

**Cover the sown seeds** with plastic or a damp towel, and let the seeds germinate at room temperature. **Place the container** under grow lights as soon as there's sign of growth. Water it with a spray bottle. Don't let the soil dry out, but don't drown it either.

**Water with liquid organic fertilizer** after two or three weeks. Leave two weeks between fertilizing.

**Harvest** when the leaves are 2" to 4" (5 to 10 cm) tall, and preferably stagger your harvest. This provides leftover plants with more space and strength to grow.

## SPROUT SUPERFOODS

During the hippie era in the '70s, we sprouted everything we could. Later on many of us stopped, and didn't even think of sprouting as a form of cultivation. But I've given sprouting another try. Sprouting is a record-breaking growth method. It only needs water, heat, and oxygen to kick-start the process, which in turn produces a harvest within a few days.

Also, sprouts are horrendously expensive in grocery stores, and they aren't always fresh. If you grow your own sprouts, your harvest will be cheaper and better.

When you soak seeds (even peas and beans) overnight, they'll absorb water. This awakens the enzymes needed to make the seeds sprout. Once the sprout grows, all the vitamins, minerals, and antioxidants—well, everything healthy that was destined for the growing plant—become accessible to us. We have in effect turned a dry and lifeless seed into a superfood.

### HOW CAN WE USE SPROUTS?

Sprouts used to be heaped onto a plate or in a sandwich. We've learned from Asian and Indian cuisine to use sprouts in spring rolls, soups, stir-fries, samosas, and stews. And inspiration has also reached us via the raw food community, where sprouts are often used in wraps or smoothies.

If you want to keep things simple, sprinkle sprouts on all of the foods you wish to enrich with vitamins and freshness.

*Right: Microgreens are grown in plastic containers from the grocery store. Pierce holes at the bottom, and line with a double layer of paper towels.*

Or, stuff flatbread full of alfalfa sprouts or other tender sprouts. The heap of sprouts in a sandwich is still a tasty option.

The larger seed sprouts—those from peas, lentils, and smaller beans—are best for cooking. Sprouting decreases the cooking time by a lot, and the flavor is fresher.

## WHAT CAN BE SPROUTED?

Most seeds from edible plants can be sprouted, as long as they have not been shelled. However, the largest seeds, i.e., large beans, take far too long to sprout to make them worth it. Itty-bitty seeds can also be sprouted, but they're worth more grown as microgreens. This is true for, say, amaranth, garden cress, and chia seeds.

Mung and alfalfa sprouts are the most common type of sprouts found in grocery stores. Mung beans are super-tasty and wonderful to snack on. It's also the only legume you can sprout and eat directly after sprouting. This is because the lectins—which are toxic—in the mung bean disappear when the mung bean sprouts. Other legumes need to be parboiled and cooked for the lectins to break down, otherwise you may suffer digestive upset.

In the table on p. 146 I show which vegetables and herbs work best for sprouting. Check the yields column to know how much seed to use. Broccoli seeds, for example, increase five-fold when they sprout. So a scant ½ cup (1 dl) of seeds will yield a little over 2 cups of sprouts.

You'll find suitable seeds in well-stocked grocery stores as well as in health food stores. Sometimes the package will tell if you can sprout the seeds, but occasionally it doesn't. And please, don't make my mistake and buy shelled pumpkin and sunflower seeds. They won't sprout, of course.

## A SALMONELLA THREAT?

Sprouts can make you sick—that's a fact. It happens often because sprouts are contaminated somewhere along the chain of production. In 1994, 278 people in Sweden were infected with the salmonella bacteria. The cause of the outbreak turned out to be alfalfa sprouts purchased at a grocery store. Contamination can also occur due to a growing process gone wrong, like if the temperature was too high. Heat, in tandem with humidity, can promote bacterial growth.

When growing your own sprouts you want to be extra careful about contamination. You can avoid it because you have control over the entire process. Good hygiene—i.e., keeping growing containers and hands clean—is the best way to ensure no bacterial growth happens. It's important to rinse the sprouts frequently—at least two to three times every 24 hours—and to make sure excess water always drains off. You can pasteurize the seeds if you want to feel extra sure about them not being contaminated; you do this by immersing them in 185°F (85°C) water for 25 to 30 seconds. Do not do it longer, as this might render the seeds nonviable. Soak and sprout the seeds as usual afterwards.

## THREE SPROUTING METHODS

**Sprout in a sprouting tower;** they're available in health food stores, among other places (see picture on the next page), and they're great. They're made from plastic trays that are stacked on top of each other. All have perforated bottoms that allow excess water to continuously drain out.

**Sprout in a glass jar,** which holds about 2 to 4 ¼ cups (½ to 1 liter). Instead of using a lid, stretch a net or a square of cheesecloth across the opening, and secure it with a rubber band. That way

*Left: Tender leaves are grown in soil; the deeper the soil, the larger the leaves. For the leaves in the picture, the soil depth was approximately 1 ¼" (3 cm).*

you can easily rinse the sprouts and drain out the water. Place the jar upside down and leaning slightly so all excess water runs out.

**Sprout in a bag**. Sew or buy a bag made from a thin, porous fabric. The bag should hold about 4 ¼ cups (1 liter). It's good if you can tighten it at the top with some ribbon. Hang the bag—above the sink is handy—during sprouting. When you've rinsed the bag under the tap, hang the bag up again so the excess water drains off. This method is good for peas, beans, and lentils.

### THIS IS HOW YOU SPROUT

**Soak** the seeds in at least 3 to 4 times their volume in water; you can never have too much water. The

*When left to my own devices, I will use a sprouting tower, which you can typically find in health food stores.*

seeds will only absorb the water they need. Pour off any debris that floats to the surface and fill up with fresh water. Repeat this process until the water is clean. Soak the seeds for approximately 12 hours. By all means, change the water once during soaking. Pour off all the water after soaking.

**Choose a sprouting container:** Select a plastic sprouting tower, glass jars, or bags, and then spread the seeds. If you want to know the amount of seed you'll need, check the table on p.146. Avoid sprouting in sunlight.

**Rinse** at least once a day, and make sure the water drains off after each rinse.

**Do a taste test** before you harvest: Some like long sprouts, while others prefer short and plump sprouts. You can also check the table on p. 146, which lists approximate times for sprouting. Expose your sprouts to daylight for a few days if you wish to load them with chlorophyll.

**Finish off** with one or two rinses and let all water drain off. The sprouts must be absolutely dry, as dampness will quickly ruin them. Store the sprouts in a plastic bag in the refrigerator. They will keep for about a week, but are best eaten within two to three days.

### HERBS AND CHILI PEPPERS

Nurseries often sell pots of thyme, lemon balm, mint, rosemary, oregano, sage, French tarragon, and other perennial herbs, even in winter. They make excellent potted plants during the colder months, but they also need extra help with grow lights. You can grow them from seed, of course, but then you won't be able to harvest them until their second year.

Another option is to buy plants at the grocery store. You buy small pots, harvest two-thirds of

*Beans and peas can be sprouted in hanging bags. Place the bag under the water tap when rinsing.*

the herb, and plant the rest in your indoor garden, where they will soon grow and start to produce. Two birds with one stone! And since we don't use lots of herbs, one pot for each plant should be enough.

For one plant, you'll need a regular clay pot approximately 6" (15 cm) in diameter. But it will look fuller if you plant three to a pot measuring 7 ¾" (20 cm) in diameter.

Then, water sparingly. The biggest threat is not drought but rot. Water in liquid fertilizer every other week after three weeks. Use only half the dose recommended on the bottle. Harvest the plant as needed.

The herbs can spend their future in your garden or on your balcony, if you can keep them alive until spring. But they require watered-in fertilizer, just like potted plants. Thyme, sage, and rosemary are watered more sparingly than herb-like spices.

I'm more than happy to add a pot of green garlic stalks, which are nicer than chives, to my herbs. Push garlic cloves in soil in a regular clay pot. The pointy end faces up and can peak over the soil's surface by about a ¼" (1 cm). Harvest the leaves in successive batches.

You can also spoil yourself with a potted chili pepper during the winter; the peppers are hot and tasty. But this means you will have to manage to overwinter the plants, or that you have a well-stocked nursery nearby.

## HYDROPONICS—WATER GARDENING

Who would have believed that a soil lover like myself would get myself a hydro-culture (also known as hydroponics) setup? It's a type of soilless garden, and I do have one now. A comforting chugging can be heard from the water-filled plastic box thanks to the aquarium pump that drives oxygen into the nutrient-filled solution from which the plants get their food.

The mizuna cabbage and the basil growing there at the moment are just as splendid as if they were in the garden beds outside. All the same, the most incredible thing about them is their roots. Wow, are they BIG! The extraordinary sturdy root growth is typical of hydro-culture, and when the roots are big, the plants grow extremely fast.

Just as when they're in outside garden beds, these plants don't just require nutrients but oxygen, too. Oxygenation is vital in hydro-culture. If the plants don't get enough oxygen the roots will rot. You solve this problem by using an aquarium pump and what is known as a marine air stone.

Commercial enterprises regularly grow in hydro-culture with nutrient-rich solutions, and home gardeners are adopting this method as

**145**

**Sprouters' favorites.**

| PLANT | SPROUT, IN DAYS | ½ CUP SEED YIELDS | USE |
|---|---|---|---|
| Adzuki beans | 3–4 | Approx. 1 cup | For the epicure. Always eat cooked. In soups, stews, etc. |
| Alfalfa | 5–6 | Approx. 3 cups | Mild, pea-like flavor. Used as a salad, and is never cooked. |
| Fenugreek | 4–6 | Approx. 2 cups | Curry flavor! Sprinkle over Indian dishes, or mix with mild leaves. Be aware that you'll smell of fenugreek after you've eaten them. |
| Broccoli | 3–6 | Approx. 2 cups | Somewhat peppery in flavor, like radish sprouts, but a bit chewier. They're best fresh, as a salad or side dish. |
| Green lentils | 2–3 | Approx. 1 cup | Tasty in salad or soup, for example. Only needs to be cooked for a few minutes. |
| Chickpeas | 3–4 | Approx. 1 cup | Harvested when the sprout is very short. Fine, nutty flavor. Best prepared by cooking for 5 minutes, or roasted in a frying pan. |
| Mung beans | 3–5 | Approx. 1 cup | Used in noodle soups, spring rolls, stir-fries, salads, etc. Wonderfully nutty and crisp. Used both fresh and cooked. This is a clear favorite! |
| Radish | 3–6 | Approx. 2 cups | Somewhat peppery flavor. Sprinkle over Asian dishes or use in a salad. |
| Peas | 2–3 | Approx. 1 cup | Taste best in salad or as a snack. The flavor is almost like fresh peas. |

well. It's a bit more complicated than growing in paper towels or in soil, and it demands a few hundred dollars investment and some minor woodworking skills.

However, after that's done, the rest is simple as well as economical. Pest attacks are far and few between, which is awesome. We even dodge fungus gnats. And, we don't have to buy soil and cart it home.

You can grow all types of plants with hydro-culture, even chili peppers and tomatoes. But leaves work best. They yield the biggest haul per square foot.

A hydro-culture setup can have many different looks. The one that works best for beginners is called DWC, or Deep Water Culture. Basically, it's a plastic box that's filled with water and topped by a lid. Net pots containing plants hang from the lid, and the plant roots go into the nutrient solution. There's a lot of excellent information about the method online. In a moment, you can read a description of how I built a simple DWC.

## GOING ORGANIC OR NOT?

Special nutritional preparations are needed in hydro-culture. Not only should they contain nitrogen, phosphorus, potassium (NPK: Nitrogen,

*Chili pepper Caribbean Red growing under grow light in the window.*

Phosphorous, and Potash-Potassium), but also all trace elements that plants typically get from the soil. Aquarium supply stores might carry suitable products, but more often than not you'll find them online.

Most growers who practice hydro-culture use mineral—more commonly called inorganic—fertilizer. They work better than organic fertilizer, as the latter raises the risk of undesired growth and root rot.

Hydro-culture growers point out that mineral fertilizers are also beneficial for the environment. Very small amounts of nutrients are used, and nothing is lost because the system is a closed one. And there's also no fertilizer leakage into the groundwater, which is unavoidable with soil cultivation.

If you still prefer to use organic fertilizer, it is vital that you have a pump that runs for a few hours every day—or better yet, 24 hours a day.

For the plants to utilize the organic fertilizer, plenty of microorganisms must be present that will break down the nutrients and make it available to the plants. But those microorganisms need somewhere to live, somewhere to bond to. You can solve this problem by filling a net bag with a few quarts (a few liters) of Leca clay pebbles, and leave it in the fertilizer solution; that way the microorganisms will multiply quickly and enable the absorption of nutrients. You don't need to use this procedure if you use mineral fertilizer.

*Basil that has been grown by hydro-culture has huge leaves that are harvested in successive batches.*

- Liquid hydroponic fertilizer (organic options are available)
- An aquarium pump and marine air stone
- A timer—optional
- Grow light
- Seeds

**YOU WILL NEED:**
- A plastic box (not see-through) with a lid, approximately 7¾" to 9¾" (20 to 25 cm) deep
- A power drill with drill bit for making holes
- 6 net pots, approximately 2" to 3" (5 to 8 cm)
- Leca clay pebbles
- Starter cubes (also called rooting cubes or seedling starter cubes)

**HOW TO BUILD A HYDROPONIC STRUCTURE**
**1. Drill holes** in the lid of the plastic box with a power drill. You can buy a drill in your local DIY or hardware store. The holes must be big enough to allow the net pots to hang through them. Drill the holes (3 to 5 cm) approximately 1" to 2" apart.

*This is what you'll need when using the Deep Water Culture (DWC) hydro-culture method. Holes are drilled in the lid for the net pots.*

*Basil and mizuna cabbage grow impressive leaves and roots with the hydro-culture method.*

2. **Water** the rooting cubes and put them in the net pots. Fill with Leca pebbles so the cubes are stable. Poke a hole in the middle of the cubes and sow 2–3 seeds in each hole.

3. **Fill the box with water** and add half a dose of fertilizer. The water level must reach the bottom of the net pots. If you use organic fertilizer, place a weighted net bag with about 1 to 2 quarts (1 to 2 liters) of Leca pebbles at the bottom.

4. **Connect the pump and the marine air stone.** The marine air stone is placed at the bottom of the box. The pump will be running 15 minutes (or more) every 24 hours if you use min-

eral fertilizer. If you've organic fertilizer, let it work $^{24}/_7$, or at least several hours out of the day.

5. **Place the lid on top** and place the net pots in the holes.

6. You'll need to add grow lights **once the seeds have germinated.** At the same time, you'll need to add another half dose of fertilizer.

7. Once the plants have long white roots, **lower the water level** so the pots are hanging about an inch above the water's surface; part of the roots will still be in the nutrient-rich water.

**8. Add more fertilizer** about every 10 days. The dosage depends on the manufacturer—follow the instructions on the bottle.

**9. Change the water** if growth starts to stall, even if you've fertilized according to the instructions. You will not need to do this if everything is growing well.

## HYDROPONIC STRUCTURE

A cross-section of the hydroponic structure. Two-thirds of the root system is below the water's surface.

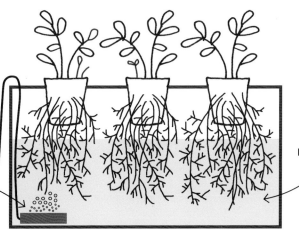

Marine air stone

Oxygen pump

Fertilized water

## THE GARDENING YEAR IS OVER AND DONE—TIME TO START ANEW!

Spring, summer, fall, and winter—the gardening season is over and I'm already planning the next one. In the southern part of Sweden, the soil is preparing itself while in the north the frost is still deeply embedded. But the spring sun is spreading its warmth everywhere.

Personally, my longing for dirt and outdoor gardening is very deep, and I choose to take a break from indoor gardening. Not from hydro-culture, however—it's far too thrilling—so I move the boxes to a sunny window. They do perfectly well there without any grow lights. At this time of year all the grow lights are used for forcing plants.

You can continue indoor gardening if you want to, even without grow lights. If you become fed up with hydro-culture, you'll have a fertilizer mix that your potted plants will love.

No, for me it's time to pull on my rubber boots. I must check if things have started to emerge in the heated cold frame! And later, I think I will sow tomatoes.

*Right: amaranth, sunflower shoots, lemon thyme (perennial), and pea shoots.*

# INDEX

Page numbers in bold indicate chapters.